"I highly recommend *Veggie Burgers Every Which Way*, a really, really wonderful veggie burger cookbook with notes on all the different kinds of ingredients and how they work . . . [it's] an in-depth veggie burger lesson."

—TEJAL RAO, *The New York Times*

"This is a terrific book! I've never been a fan of veggie burgers—neither the word 'veggie' nor the dry little disks with their strange little flavors. But Lukas Volger has just the right idea: Make real food with real flavor—and burgers that go far beyond any microwavable snack. There's a lot to like in *Veggie Burgers Every Which Way*, including some very appealing sides, dressings, and, what else? Buns! I'm headed to my kitchen right now."

—DEBORAH MADISON, author of *Vegetarian Cooking for Everyone*
and *Vegetable Literacy*

"Lukas Volger's burgers are made with real food—fresh produce, whole grains and beans, fresh herbs and spices—combined with imagination and great taste. This appealing book is the best collection of vegetarian burgers I've ever seen, a refreshing departure from the overprocessed veggie burgers of yore."

—MARTHA ROSE SHULMAN, Recipes for Health, nytimes.com,
and author of *The Simple Art of Vegetarian Cooking*

*

"The world of burgers has just grown bigger, fresher, more colorful, and deliciously diverse thanks to Lukas Volger's back-to-basics approach to the veggie burger. Summer barbecues may never look the same again!"

—CATHY ERWAY, James Beard Award–winning food writer and author

"Vegans and vegetarians (and others eating meatless) often resort to cooking frozen veggie burgers out of a box . . . [with *Veggie Burgers Every Which Way*], you can whip up the real deal: great-tasting colorful homemade variations with fresh produce, whole grains, beans, rice, bread crumbs, spices, and herbs. They will be as good as the ingredients that go into them . . . Appealing topping, side, dressing and bun options are included, too."

—LOS ANGELES DAILY NEWS

✻

"One of Volger's best veggie burgers combines a variety of mushrooms and barley, combining foresty and nutty flavors you'd find in a wintertime wild mushroom soup . . . Try going back to eating one of those frozen soy burgers after that."

—THE OREGONIAN

✻

"Volger's excellent new book, *Veggie Burgers Every Which Way*, should not be thought of as just for vegetarians . . . it is the variety and creativity of the recipes that makes this new cookbook stand out. Recipes such as his Tuscan White Bean Burger . . . are sure to get just about any carnivore's mouth watering."

—CBC NEWS

✻

"Who knew shredded carrots or quinoa could be so deliciously molded into a pattie? And satisfy a dyed-in-the-wool carnivore."

—PITTSBURGH POST-GAZETTE

✻

"This is a small volume with a big mission: to up the flavor profile of this particular vegetarian genre."

—WASHINGTON POST

✻

"Lukas Volger . . . elevates the vegetarian burger to its rightful status as real food."

—MONTREAL GAZETTE

Also by Lukas Volger

Snacks for Dinner: Small Bites, Full Plates, Can't Lose

Start Simple: Eleven Everyday Ingredients for Countless Weeknight Meals

Bowl: Vegetarian Recipes for Ramen, Pho, Bibimbap,
Dumplings, and Other One-Dish Meals

Vegetarian Entrées That Won't Leave You Hungry:
Nourishing, Flavorful Main Courses That Fill the Center of the Plate

VEGGIE BURGERS

every which way

Fresh, Flavorful & Healthy Plant-Based Burgers

REVISED & UPDATED SECOND EDITION

LUKAS VOLGER

Photography by Evi Abeler

THE EXPERIMENT

NEW YORK

VEGGIE BURGERS EVERY WHICH WAY: *Fresh, Flavorful, and Healthy Plant-Based Burgers—Revised and Updated Second Edition*
Copyright © 2010, 2023 by Lukas Volger
Photographs, including cover photograph, copyright © 2023 by Evi Abeler
Photographs on pages xiv, 13, 33, 47, 55, 65, 66, 69, 75, 80, 84, 87, 97, 111, 112, 115, 126, 129, 135, 138, 140, 150, and 157 copyright © 2010 by Christina Heaston
Photographs on pages 109 and 139 copyright © 2010 by Sean Dougherty
Photograph on page 153 copyright © by The Experiment, LLC
Additional photographs copyright © by Adobe Stock

Originally published by The Experiment, LLC, in 2010. This revised and updated edition first published in 2023.

The Experiment, LLC
220 East 23rd Street, Suite 600
New York, NY 10010-4658
theexperimentpublishing.com

This book contains the opinions and ideas of its author. It is intended to provide helpful and informative material on the subjects addressed in the book. It is sold with the understanding that the author and publisher are not engaged in rendering medical, health, or any other kind of personal professional services in the book. The author and publisher specifically disclaim all responsibility for any liability, loss, or risk—personal or otherwise—that is incurred as a consequence, directly or indirectly, of the use and application of any of the contents of this book.

THE EXPERIMENT and its colophon are registered trademarks of The Experiment, LLC. Many of the designations used by manufacturers and sellers to distinguish their products are claimed as trademarks. Where those designations appear in this book and The Experiment was aware of a trademark claim, the designations have been capitalized.

The Experiment's books are available at special discounts when purchased in bulk for premiums and sales promotions as well as for fund-raising or educational use. For details, contact us at info@theexperimentpublishing.com.

Library of Congress Cataloging-in-Publication Data

Names: Volger, Lukas, author. | Abeler, Evi, photographer.
Title: Veggie burgers every which way : fresh, flavorful, and healthy
plant-based burgers—revised and updated second edition / Lukas Volger ; photography by Evi Abeler.
Description: Second edition. | New York, NY : The
   Experiment, [2023] | Includes index.
Identifiers: LCCN 2023003961 (print) | LCCN 2023003962 (ebook) | ISBN
   9781615199846 | ISBN 9781615199853 (ebook)
Subjects: LCSH: Meat substitutes. | Hamburgers. | Vegetarian cooking.
Classification: LCC TX838 .V65 2023 (print) | LCC TX838 (ebook) | DDC
   641.5/636--dc23/eng/20230201
LC record available at https://lccn.loc.gov/2023003961
LC ebook record available at https://lccn.loc.gov/2023003962

ISBN 978-1-61519-984-6
Ebook ISBN 978-1-61519-985-3

Cover and text design, and photograph on page 153, by Beth Bugler
Food styling by Albane Sharrard

Manufactured in China

First printing June 2023
10 9 8 7 6 5 4 3 2 1

In memory of my mom, Pam Volger

Contents

Ⓥ = vegan   ⒼⒻ = gluten-free

Preface

What can be said now, about veggie burgers, that couldn't have been said in 2010, when the first edition of this book was published? Though veggie burgers were nothing new at that time, it seemed then that they still had something to prove. At my book events and online, I'd have people say, "Call it what you like—but it's not a *burger*." (I always wondered if these people had the same linguistic bone to pick [pun intended] with lamb burgers, shrimp burgers, salmon burgers, chicken burgers, and bison burgers.) I haven't encountered that line of argument in a while, which I'll take as progress.

More broadly, I could never have predicted that veggie burgers would soon "bleed," or that they'd take hold of the popular imagination, or that such an innovation would even see the light of day. But here we are, and I truly think it's a good thing. Veggie burgers aren't just a fixture of Western food culture; in many ways they've come to embody the future of food, particularly in terms of how food tech and entrepreneurial efforts are envisioning ways to combat climate change, factory farming, and the ethics of eating meat.

That said, I've never been very excited about a veggie burger that tastes like meat. My perspective in this book was, and continues to be, that veggie burgers should be creative expressions of vegetables. After all, I'm in this business because I love vegetables, love my local farmers market, and love eating with the seasons. In my view, vegetables should be the star player, and veggie burgers can be a vessel for the flavor of carrots, kale, or beets when they're fresh and delicious, and be presented in a format that's new and unexpected. I don't know about you, but to me that's more fun and also more appetizing.

In the years after *Veggie Burgers Every Which Way* was first published, I started a small food business, a line of retail veggie burgers called Made by Lukas. Through that project, I doubled down on this concept of vegetable-forward veggie burgers. The tagline was "veggie burgers should taste like vegetables," and they were sold as veggie burger "mixes," to be thought of like ground meat in that you can shape them into whatever size burger you please and cook them off to order. They were 80 percent vegetables, and ultimately available in three flavors: Beet, Carrot-Parsnip, and Kale.

Made by Lukas lasted for about four years, which was long enough to learn how difficult running a food business built upon a product that's unfamiliar (it's much easier to sell something that customers already know how to use, I soon found out) and perishable (grocery stores prefer a shelf life of three months to three weeks) would be. But rather than a lab, those recipes were born in my own home kitchen, just like these original recipes were, and I never shared them. I'm so pleased to finally have a place to offer them, and also pleased to be reminded how home-cook friendly the recipes actually are. I've also added a few other burgers and recipes that I've been tinkering with and enjoying over the years, since my appetite and interest obviously didn't end when the first edition of this book was published.

Writing a book is a funny experience, since it's something that's permanent and doesn't easily lend itself to updates and revisions the way that the living document of the internet—or even one's own recipe collections, with their notes and annotations—can. A printed book assumes that it's possible to fully master something, and to say all there is to say about a topic. But in the dozen-plus years since then, I've continued to learn a great deal about cooking vegetables in general, and veggie burgers in particular. My thinking has evolved just as they, as their own category of food, have evolved.

While my original recipes in the first edition relied more heavily on egg as a binder, these new ones are mostly vegan and even gluten-free, and in the updated front matter of this book, I've shared some of the tips I've learned over the past dozen years for adapting along those lines. (Hopefully these latest methods and techniques will provide you the tools you need to start creating veggie burgers of your own!) But aside from the few tweaks to some of the original recipes, such as streamlining them in ways that didn't occur to me until after publication, or making a few small ingredient improvements, I've tried to keep the soul of the original recipes the same.

Lastly, while I enjoyed and had opinions about veggie burgers prior to writing *Veggie Burgers Every Which Way*, I owe huge thanks to The Experiment publisher, Matthew Lore, for entrusting me to realize his idea for this book. It fully unlocked a real passion—and helped to launch a career for me.

I hope you enjoy these recipes, new and old ones alike, and that they continue to find a place in your everyday cooking. And while the cultural rise of the veggie burger should give you some hope for the future, I hope that the pro-vegetable, eating-with-the-seasons spirit that infuses this book is just as alluring.

—Lukas Volger, 2023

Introduction

Why bother making veggie burgers when it's so easy to buy them in boxes? A veggie burger is no mere approximation of a hamburger. Aside from their shared circular shapes, the two have very little in common. So why is it that veggie burgers are so often used as boring stand-ins for hamburgers? And why do we call them "burgers" in the first place? It seems that veggie burgers have been unfairly represented, and it's about time to champion them as their own independent category of food.

Over the past few decades, packaged and frozen veggie burgers have developed a loyal following among vegetarians and vegans, and I'm frequently baffled as to how this happened. I'm a longtime veggie burger enthusiast, but I've never been a fan of those. I don't like the rubbery texture, and I don't like all the salt and the often-cryptic ingredients—can someone tell me what modified vegetable gum is, or autolyzed yeast extract? Can I buy either of them at the grocery store? Most of all, I don't like that processed flavor, present even in the ones that claim to be made only from identifiable ingredients; I find it to be suggestive of fast-food joints and stinky microwaves. It seems that most people settle for these as a quick fix: as a snack, an easy dinner, or something to pop in the microwave on your lunch break. When I talked to vegetarians and vegans as I was working on this book, even accomplished cooks admitted that it had never occurred to them to make veggie burgers themselves—despite eating them for years. Many, however, told me of their favorite store-bought brands and the restaurants that serve the best renditions. Now, I've long known that veggie burgers have a central role in the diets of vegetarians and vegans (and many omnivores as well), but I didn't realize how limited our collective curiosity appears to be when it comes to this particular staple.

In 1982, Gregory Sams, a British nutritionist and entrepreneur, patented the first "VegeBurger," which was a dry mix packet, and in the spirit of convenience, new styles have appeared in grocery stores ever since. Because many of us want to know exactly what is in the food we eat, where it originates, how it's been prepared, and what its environmental and ethical toll is. At the same time, hamburgers continue to reign as our easiest calories, a mentality that likely reflects a culture that has grown accustomed to easy-access, high-calorie, fast food. After all, you can get a hamburger without having to park your car. And in the tradition of the classic barbecue or cookout, just throw a few burgers and hot dogs on the grill, grab a tub of potato salad, a watermelon, some beer and soda, and eat to your heart's content. This is where, I think, veggie burgers asserted themselves: as a peace offering. Here, someone might have said, flopping what looked like a frozen hockey puck on the grill, we wouldn't want you to feel left out. Because when we

think of veggie burgers, these are often the terms, even for those of us who've been eating them for practically our entire lives. We don't eat them because we like them, per se; we eat them because it's a way we can take part in the culinary custom. Veggie burgers have been treated as an afterthought to a meat-fest, and we've accepted them as some kind of consolation prize.

These frozen burgers, if not served as a "special request" alongside a spread of meats, appear rather insultingly designed to be consumed by just one person. How else to explain the individual wrappers, akin to frozen TV dinners or individually packaged, frozen burritos? It sends the message that a veggie burger isn't something that any number of people would all want to eat at the same time, that one would never be inclined to serve a veggie burger at a dinner party, or, worse yet: You wouldn't want to eat that in public!

No more, I say! A hearty, delicious, easy, homemade veggie burger is within your reach! And there's more good news: I have collected here over thirty-five of them to choose from. And your friends will want to eat them, too—even the ones who eat meat.

From the beginning of my interest in veggie burgers, my approach has been to regard the veggie burger as a cuisine unto itself: It is far more varied than its meat-based counterpart and ungoverned by any particular geographic cuisine or generally accepted set of rules. The veggie burger is a very accepting category of food. Which brings up the question: What is a veggie burger, then, besides something that is meatless and shaped like a disk? I'll show rather than tell, by sharing a few examples: Curried Eggplant and Tomato Burgers (page 86), Baked Quinoa Burgers (page 54), Spinach-Chickpea Burgers (page 81), Spiced Lentil Burgers (page 32), Spicy Peanut and Carrot Burgers (page 67), Beet and Brown Rice Burgers (page 64). What these burgers have in common is that they are all unique expressions of the colors, textures, and tastes of the assorted fresh ingredients from which they are prepared—and that they started out as seeds in the ground.

Use the freshest vegetables and ingredients you can get your hands on, whether purchased at the farmers' market, delivered in your weekly CSA box, grown in your backyard, picked up at a produce stand along the highway, or selected from the produce aisle of your grocery store. Your veggie burgers will only be as good as the ingredients that go into them. As I'll explain briefly in the next chapter, I prefer to use organic "whole foods" as frequently as possible: ingredients that have been fussed with the least before they come into my possession (minimally processed, unrefined).

I've been eating veggie burgers since college—and thinking consciously about them for almost as long. *Veggie Burgers Every Which Way* assembles literally every veggie burger I can think of—as well as a few that other cooks have dreamt up. You might be surprised by some of the unconventional burgers found here. Try the gluten-free Beet "Tartare" (page 70), or Fava Bean Burgers (page 49), or the delicious vegan Tofu and Chard Burgers (page 96) for some surprising spins. Or if you want to keep things more conventional, I suggest the vegan Chipotle Black Bean Burgers (page 92), the "Garden" Burgers (page 101; the closest approximation of a store-bought burger that I've concocted), or the Pub Grub Veggie Burgers (page 55). While you're making your own veggie burgers, I encourage you to try your hand at making your own burger buns as well; included here are both vegan recipes and a gluten-free one. There are also some delicious, healthy takes on the traditional burger sides. I could (and often do) prepare all of these recipes frequently, but the Rutabaga Fries (page 144) have become a particular favorite—and if you've not often cooked with rutabagas, they may be a revelation. In the end, I hope—and am willing to bet—you'll no longer have the impulse to reach for the frozen package.

Veggie Burger Basics

In many ways, veggie burgers are a simple endeavor: Take beans, grains, tofu, a vegetable—or a combination thereof—and, using binders and starches and complementary flavors, make the mixture malleable and form it into patties. The trick is to get the balance right. Too many bread crumbs, for example, will wash out the flavor; too few and you run the risk of the burger squeezing out the other end of the bun when you bite into it. The recipes in this book will produce a flavorful burger that will hold its shape. In this chapter I'll expand on a few of the principles behind the recipes.

Ingredients

BEANS

Beans are an essential ingredient in many of these recipes. There are hundreds of types of beans on the market, including an ever-growing category of heirloom beans. I'm willing to bet that all of them would be good in a veggie burger, and I encourage you to seek them out and try cooking with them. On page 28, I go into greater detail about the types of beans used in this book and their various merits in veggie burger recipes.

Canned beans are on many occasions a necessary shortcut—since using canned beans is, by leaps and bounds, less time-consuming than cooking your own. However, I urge you to at least have the intention of cooking your own beans every now and then.

Cooking with dried beans does take some time. Most beans benefit from having a day to soak, and sometimes they can take up to a few hours to cook. But the time beans require isn't active time—most of the cooking and soaking doesn't even require your supervision. And what can I say to make you believe me when I say the flavor of dried beans cooked at home is far superior to the flavor of canned beans—even the best canned beans? You might be surprised to find that properly home-cooked beans are supple and tender and hold their shape well, unlike the filmy, sometimes watery ones that so often come out of a can; they have a clean, distinctive flavor.

If you are going to use canned beans, I urge you to spend the extra sixty cents or so on an organic, sodium-free, better-quality brand. In my experience, organic is better than not organic. As the organic farming and food-production companies become even more industrialized, one certainly can't just accept this as a fail-safe rule. (And, as is sometimes worth pointing out, organic does not always mean healthier!) But I do find that organic foods taste better, and I rest easier knowing that they haven't been doused in chemicals and fertilizers.

Whatever the canned beans you use, be sure to rinse them thoroughly: cover with water in a large bowl and rub the beans gently with your fingers so as to thoroughly clean them of the liquid they were canned in, then drain.

A NOTE ABOUT CANNED BEANS: One 14-ounce (400 g) can of beans yields roughly 1½ cups (270 g) beans.

Cooking Dried Beans

Begin by combing through them for small stones, immature or overdry beans, and other debris—I don't often find these kinds of things, but when I do find a stone, it feels like a blessing because it means I've spared myself or one of my dining companions from chipping a tooth.

By rinsing, soaking, and refreshing the water you are also removing some of the starches that cause gas. There is some contention on this matter, though. Some science supports that changing the soaking and cooking water is effective, while others advocate adding a sprig of epazote (a leafy herb native to Central America and used frequently in Mexican cuisine), or combining beans with rhizomes, kombu, or other spices and herbs while they are cooking. Others think an over-the-counter solution like Bean-O is a perfectly fine solution. My personal feeling is that everyone reacts to beans differently, and the biggest culprit of bean-related indigestion is undercooked beans and frankly, I think folks need to just relax on this issue and focus on cooking their beans well.

There are two soaking methods (but if you're pressed for time, you can always skip soaking).

* **OVERNIGHT SOAK:** In a large bowl, cover the beans by three to four times their volume with water (the beans will double to triple in volume, and you want to ensure that they do not rise above the water level during the soak); let stand overnight. The next day, drain off the water, rinse the beans, and proceed with cooking.

* **QUICK(ER) SOAK:** Place the beans in the cooking pot with water three to four times their volume. Bring the water to a boil and boil the beans for a couple minutes. Remove from the heat, cover the pot, and let stand for at least 1 hour, or up to 4 hours. When the soak is done, drain off the water, rinse the beans, and proceed with cooking.

Or, skip the soak. If the only thing stopping you from cooking a pot of beans is the time it takes to soak them, skip the soaking. The fresher the beans are, the less likely they'll need soaking. You'll just need to add some additional cooking time.

You can cook the beans on the stovetop, or in a pressure cooker or slow cooker.

* **TO COOK ON THE STOVETOP:** Place the beans in a pot covered with water by three or four times their volume. Add about 2 tablespoons of olive oil and any aromatics you please (half an onion, a few sage leaves, bay leaf, garlic). Bring to a boil. Reduce the heat to a gentle simmer, partially cover, and cook the beans until tender. Start salting the beans after about 20 minutes of cooking. The beans may take as little as 30 minutes to cook, or they could take 90 minutes—let your taste buds be your guide.

* **TO COOK IN A PRESSURE COOKER:** Place the soaked beans in your pressure cooker (or Instant Pot) and cover with water by three to four times their volume. Add about 2 tablespoons of olive oil and any aromatics you please (half an onion, a few sage leaves, bay leaf, garlic) as well as 1 tablespoon salt. Cook on high pressure for

18 minutes, then allow natural release for 15 minutes. Check for doneness—you may need to pressure cook the beans for another 5 to 10 minutes if they aren't tender, following the same instructions here using natural release. Add additional salt to taste.

* **TO COOK IN A SLOW COOKER:** Place the soaked beans in your slow cooker (or Instant Pot) and cover with water by three to four times their volume. Add about 2 tablespoons of olive oil and any aromatics you please (half an onion, a few sage leaves, bay leaf, garlic) as well as 1 tablespoon salt. Cook for 5 hours, or until the beans are tender. Depending on the bean, you may need to cook for an additional hour. Add additional salt to taste.

* **LEFTOVERS:** A bowl of warm, freshly cooked beans drizzled with olive oil and a sprinkling of salt and pepper is one of my favorite snacks. Also, I can find uses for almost any leftover beans in salads, soups, and as spreads for sandwiches. And don't toss the broth! It functions great as soup stock or accompaniment to cooked beans, and when it's perfectly savory and flavorful, it's a delicious thing to sip on its own.

Store leftover beans in their cooking liquid in an airtight container. They will keep in the refrigerator for up to a week or in the freezer for three months.

RICE

Rice is used in many of the recipes here to stretch the base vegetable, bean, or other protein and to give the burgers body and texture. Many types of rice are delicious and any variety will work for these recipes (except, perhaps, super starchy varieties like arborio and carnaroli rice, which are used to make risotto), but my default is brown rice. I use either short grain brown rice or long grain brown jasmine rice. But use what you've got, particularly if you have leftover cooked rice on hand.

Cooking Rice

✳ **WASH AND RINSE YOUR RICE:** Rice is part of a plant, just like your vegetables from the farmers market, and therefore it should be washed. Simply cover it with 1 inch (2.5 cm) of water in your cooking vessel, swish it around a few times, and drain. When cooking white rice, I repeat this process twice more to rinse the grains of excess starch, but for brown rice this isn't necessary.

✳ **COMBINE WITH WATER, AND SOAK IF YOU HAVE TIME:** The ratio of rice to water is 1:1½ for white rice and 1:2 for brown rice. Combine the rice and measured water in a heavy-bottomed saucepan, and soak for 1 to 6 hours. Like beans, this can make the rice more digestible but, in my opinion, it improves the finished result. But I don't always have the time.

✳ **TO COOK IN A RICE COOKER:** These days, this is my favorite way to cook rice. In fact, this little appliance is one of the most-used devices in my kitchen. I combine my rinsed rice and the measured water, let it soak for a few hours if I have time, then simply press "Start." It keeps a pot of rice warm for a whole day, forming the base for all types of meals in addition to veggie burgers. One note, though: Don't toss the measuring cup that comes with your rice cooker—use that exclusively for measuring your rice. Most rice cookers are manufactured in China or Japan, where 1 cup measures 180 milliliters, which is about 25 percent less volume than US cup.

✳ **TO COOK ON THE STOVETOP:** Combine your rice and measured water in a small or medium saucepan and place over medium-high heat. When the water comes to a boil, turn the heat down as low as possible and cover the pot with a tight-fitting lid. It's important that the steam doesn't escape during cooking—if you don't have a snug fit, seal the pot first with a sheet of aluminum foil and then place the lid on top of it. Cook the brown rice for 30 minutes, or white rice for 18 minutes. Remove from the heat, fluff with a fork, and let stand, covered, for at least 10 minutes before eating.

VARIATION: BOILED RICE

Boiling rice can eliminate the need to measure out water and also has the benefit of cooking brown rice in about half the time.

Bring a pot of water to boil (you need not measure the water, as long as it generously exceeds the volume of the rice). Add rice and cook for 10 to 15 minutes, until tender. Drain thoroughly.

BREAD CRUMBS

In nonvegetarian cooking, bread crumbs help aerate ground meats, to keep them from becoming too dense. The same is true of veggie burgers. While no one wants a veggie burger that is mostly bread, the starch is a necessary element. Unseasoned, store-bought bread crumbs are fine to use, but because of their coarser texture, I prefer panko to fine bread crumbs.

But if you often have bread around, it can be easy (and money-saving) to keep stale bread in a bag in your freezer, and once it's full, whip up a batch of bread crumbs. I don't bother to trim the crusts off and am completely impartial when it comes to what goes into the bag—pita bread, rolls, buns, white bread, baguette, whole wheat bread, etc. When the bag is full, I make bread crumbs.

Making Bread Crumbs

Four standard slices of bread yield about 1 cup (60 g) bread crumbs.

Preheat the oven to 325°F (165°C). Tear the bread into roughly ½-inch (1.25 cm) pieces and pulse in a food processor until ground. Transfer to a baking sheet and cook in the oven for 15 to 20 minutes, until uniformly golden, dried out, and crisp. Carefully stir the crumbs every 5 to 10 minutes (stir more frequently if your oven has uneven heat). Bread crumbs can be kept for weeks in an airtight container or even longer in the freezer.

NOTE: If you don't have a food processor, tear the bread into pieces as small as possible and then dry them out in the preheated oven. When cool, place the toasted pieces in a sturdy, airtight bag, and place the bag flat between a sandwich of kitchen towels. Grind them into crumbs up by going over them with a rolling pin, flipping the bag and shaking it periodically. Another trick for making bread crumbs that I enjoy is grating stale bread using a box grater.

Adapting for Wheat- and Gluten-Free Burgers

Gluten-free (GF) bread crumbs sold at grocery stores are often not much more than rice flour or corn meal, thus lacking the "aerating" properties of wheat-based bread. I wasn't impressed with the results I had when using these store-bought GF bread crumbs. There are some newer products out there, made from nuts or seeds, and they can be used in veggie burgers, though because they don't really absorb liquid the same way that bread does, they can sometimes result in a dense and heavy burger. For best results, I find that grinding and toasting crumbs from store-bought gluten-free breads is your best bet (just follow the instructions on page 17). Homemade gluten-free bread crumbs can be substituted in any of the recipes here that call for bread crumbs.

One of my favorite newer discoveries, which came to me as I was developing my Made by Lukas recipes, is dehydrated potato flakes. These are the same thing as "instant mashed potatoes" that you may have eaten on occasion while growing up—potatoes that have been cooked and then dried out and flaked, so that, when combined with warm liquid, they resemble freshly cooked potatoes. They expand and lightly aerate a veggie burger when used as a binder. When shopping, look for an ingredient list that is only "dehydrated potatoes"—lots of brands have other things added for flavor and as preservative. Bob's Red Mill is my favorite brand.

Another alternative, one I learned from Joni Moreno's wonderful book *More with Less*, is to cook small, fluffy grains like quinoa or millet (this works best when you have leftover quinoa on hand, in which case it's already started to dry up), then dry them out in a 300°F (150°C) oven, which will take 20 to 30 minutes. These have the extra advantage of being more nutritionally dense than standard bread crumbs.

But I've included many recipes here that are gluten-free by their very nature. As anyone who adheres to a gluten-free diet knows, there are many, many alternative flours out there that are made from beans, nuts, and grains. Flours—particularly specialty flours and gluten-free flour blends—can have significantly longer shelf lives if they are stored in the refrigerator or freezer. Transfer the flour to an airtight container and refrigerate or freeze and it will keep for months. I find that mason jars work well for this purpose. If you can find a store that sells dry goods in bulk, you'll save yourself space and money by purchasing only what you need.

> TIP: Alternative flours are often expensive, especially considering that many recipes require only small amounts. With any bean or grain flour, you can easily make your own. Grind small portions of uncooked whole seeds, nuts, or grains in a clean, dry spice grinder or high-speed blender and sift out the large chunks.

A NOTE ABOUT WHEAT AND GLUTEN-FREE

If you adhere to a gluten-free diet, you are probably highly adept at reading food labels. I've made efforts to mark which items need their gluten-free counterparts, but please use your own experience, instincts, and knowledge when shopping for ingredients.

If you're new to gluten and wheat-free eating, here is a brief summary: People who are on a GF diet are split into a few camps. First, there are those who have been diagnosed with celiac disease, a genetically determined disease in which any gluten consumed injures the lining of the small intestine and makes digestion difficult and painful. The second camp is of people who have an allergy to wheat, and the third applies to those who have autoimmune issues around wheat. While digestion-related symptoms are also prevalent in people with wheat allergies, other allergic reactions are triggered, like skin rashes, inflammation, headaches, and nausea, and those with autoimmune issues experience joint pain or other allergy-like reactions. These reactions can range from minor to life-threatening, similar to how people respond to nut allergies.

If you're trying out a wheat-free diet for the first time, there is a wealth of information online about what foods to avoid and what types of foods can be substituted for them.

Egg Substitutes

Around a third of the recipes included here are egg- and dairy-free. Without eggs, some other kind of binder is needed to help hold the burgers together. That said, most veggie burgers, once they're cooked, will firm up a bit as they cool, and this can be a helpful way to deal with a delicate burger. The following is an incomplete list of my favorite vegan veggie burger binders.

* **STEAMED POTATO AND POTATO STARCH:** In veggie burgers, the combination of steamed potato and potato starch (or cornstarch or arrowroot) is one of my favorite egg substitutes because it contributes a pleasant flavor. But use caution: Steamed potato works as a binder but does not expand while it cooks as eggs do; if overused, potato can make the burgers wet and heavy. The addition of a small amount of potato starch helps to resolve the density problem by limiting the amount of cooked potato but making use of its binding properties.

  I prefer to use Yukon Gold potatoes because I like the flavor. To steam, peel a small potato (about 2 ounces/28 g), cut it into ½-inch (1.25 cm) pieces, and place in a steaming basket. Bring a bit of water in a small saucepan to a simmer, add the basket, and cover. Cook for 8 to 10 minutes, until the potato can be effortlessly pierced with a fork or skewer. (Alternatively, leftover roasted or boiled potatoes can be substituted.) Allow to cool slightly, then mash with a fork. Half a small potato plus 1 teaspoon potato starch is roughly the equivalent of an egg.

Most grocery stores carry potato starch, though cornstarch and arrowroot powder are interchangeable. My favorite brand is Bob's Red Mill.

* **GROUND FLAXSEED:** For the equivalent of a single egg, take 1 tablespoon flaxseed and grind to powder in a spice grinder. (Alternatively, use 2½ teaspoons ground flaxseed.) Whisk in 3 tablespoons water until it emulsifies. This isn't the strongest binder, and flax has a distinctive, grainy-grassy flavor that isn't exactly subtle. But in recipes like Seeded Edamame Burgers with Brown Rice and Apples (page 37), the additional flax flavor adds a terrific dimension.

* **BLENDED TOFU:** Firm or extra firm tofu, once it's blended up in a food processor or blender to become a paste, has some strong binding properties, particularly when combined with a starch like potato starch, cornstarch, or arrowroot powder.

* **EGG REPLACER:** There are a few brands of "egg replacer" on the market and a few of them are vegetarian only (usually because they contain gelatin or algae); be sure to check the label. Many vegan cooks swear by Ener-G Egg Replacer. I do not expressly call for egg replacer in any of the recipes here, but it is a viable alternative to eggs in the burgers.

Cooking Equipment

Making veggie burgers is not a difficult culinary endeavor, but there are a few cooking tools that make the job a bit easier. Aside from the standard batterie de cuisine (good knives; a big, heavy cutting board; mixing bowls; a spatula; etc.), the following items will come in handy.

* **SIEVE:** A sieve makes the job of cleaning beans, rice, and grains infinitely easier, especially if you can find one that fits inside a larger bowl so that the contents of the strainer can be submerged in water and then lifted out. Plastic colanders have holes that are too large for small grains and beans.

* **SALAD SPINNER:** A salad spinner makes the job of cleaning greens and leafy herbs—such as spinach, kale, chard, parsley, and cilantro—a snap. The ideal salad spinner is essentially just a colander that fits inside a larger plastic bowl and has some kind of spinning mechanism that rids the greens of water. If you choose one that does not drain water out the bottom, the bowl that the colander fits into will come in handy for submerging greens and swishing them around to clean off dirt.

* **BOX GRATER:** Grated hardy vegetables like carrots and beets produce excellent texture in veggie burgers, as you'll see in several of the recipes in this book. While I have a food processor with a grater attachment, I reach for the box grater much more often— it's just so much easier to clean. There's no need to own an expensive one, but do know that once the blades on the grates have dulled, the tool will be much more difficult— and dangerous—to use. It can be worth spending a bit more on a model that's properly sharp. The Cuisinart box grater is my favorite.

* **POTATO MASHER:** This comes in handy for mashing beans and vegetables when a fork doesn't seem to be enough for the job. I prefer a "wire" potato masher to the kind that is a flat piece of metal with perforations.

* **FOOD PROCESSOR:** Here's the bad news: For some of the burgers in this book, there isn't really a way around using a food processor. A food processor will blitz everything up with minimal effort. They come in many sizes, ranging from mini choppers to industrial-size Robot Coupes. A miniature food processor can be used for veggie burgers as long as you process in small batches. A blender is unfortunately not a great substitute because it requires too much liquid in order to get the mixture moving (you'd end up with a veggie burger smoothie). But I lived for many years without a food processor, so I understand your predicament if you don't own one. Not all the recipes here require a food processor, and where applicable, I've listed alternate preparation methods.

* **CAST-IRON SKILLET:** Cast-iron skillets are great because they are significantly less expensive than other oven-safe skillets, they heat evenly, and they improve with use, developing their own unique patina by absorbing the oils of what cooks in them. (I started developing many of the recipes in this book using a new 10-inch/25 cm cast-iron skillet, and I now have a wonderfully seasoned pan.) Cast-iron skillets come in many different sizes—anywhere from 6 to 18 inches (15–46 cm) in diameter. In addition to my 10-inch skillet, I have a small 6-inch one, which is perfect for cooking a single veggie burger. But in general I get the most use out of the 10-inch skillet. Just be sure to care for your cast-iron skillet correctly: no harsh soaps, no submerging in soapy water, no scraping clean with steel wool or other abrasive sponges, unless you want to reseason your pan completely. To clean, just quickly and gently wipe out the pan using warm water and a small amount of dish soap, then blot dry with a clean towel (if left to air-dry, skillet will begin to rust).

* **NONSTICK, OVEN-SAFE SAUTÉ PAN:** Ideally all your skillets and sauté pans are oven-safe, but if you're striving to cook with less oil (I don't worry much about that here because most of these recipes are very low in fat), then the nonstick pan is the way to go. I find that it's worth spending a little extra money on these, as the better nonstick coatings last significantly longer. Look for one that has an oven-safe handle, usually made out of stainless steel. And while these are oven-safe, avoid putting them in an oven that's much hotter than 400°F (200°C)—higher heat can speed up the deterioration of the nonstick coating.

* **MEAT GRINDER:** Seriously! Well, I made veggie burgers with a friend who has a meat grinder attachment on her KitchenAid stand mixer, and it did a beautiful job of blitzing the vegetable-and-bean mixtures. By all means, don't go buy a meat grinder (much less a KitchenAid) just for this purpose. But if you have one lying around, you might discover some surprising uses for it with these recipes.

* **RICE COOKER:** I don't know why I waited so long to invite a rice cooker into my life, but when I finally did, I was shocked by how much value it brought. Many of the recipes here call for cooked rice, and when you have a rice cooker, you hardly need the foresight to cook it in advance. I have a small model made by Muji, and it works great for my small apartment kitchen.

* **FRYDADDY:** If you've any plans to deep-fry with any regularity, a FryDaddy—literally a metal bucket that plugs into an electrical socket and keeps oil at the proper 375°F (190°C) for frying—makes the job infinitely easier and cleaner. The fact that it maintains the temperature for you—no more finessing with the burner to get the oil to stay at the right temperature—is reason enough to own one. There are a few burgers here that lend themselves to deep-frying, but it's the french fries that will make the FryDaddy earn its keep.

Making Burgers

SHAPING BURGERS

I prefer my veggie burgers to be moderate in size: about 4 inches (10 cm) in diameter and ¾ inch (2 cm) thick. If you shape the burgers any larger, they become difficult to eat with a bun, and you run the risk of having them fall apart when you flip them. If they're any smaller,

they'll seem like an afterthought to the hamburger bun. That said, if you're not serving your burgers on buns, then you have much more flexibility.

Veggie burger "sliders" are also a fun variation. Simply shape rounded tablespoons of the mixture into small patties and then sauté. See note below regarding cooking time and cooking method.

COOKING METHODS

I've cooked veggie burgers in many different ways over the years: in a sauté pan, in the oven, on the barbecue, and even in the microwave on occasion. As I began to develop the recipes that appear in this book, I experimented with many different ways of cooking veggie burgers. Based on all my past experience and then my more-recent experimenting, I've settled on what I believe to be the one almost universally fail-safe method.

✳ **BEST VEGGIE BURGER COOKING METHOD:** Preheat the oven to 375°F (190°C). In an oven-safe skillet or nonstick sauté pan, heat oil over medium-high heat. When hot, add the burgers and and sear until browned on each side, turning once, 6 to 10 minutes total. Transfer the pan to the oven and bake for 12 to 15 minutes, until the burgers are firm and cooked through. If cooking a larger quantity than will fit in your skillet, brown the burgers in batches and then transfer them to a baking sheet or roasting pan before going into the oven.

This combination of first "searing" the burgers and then finishing in the oven is the same method that restaurants often use on cuts of meat. I realize it's a fairly nontraditional approach to veggie burgers. I repeatedly found that when the size of burgers I wanted to cook were cooked only in a sauté pan, they weren't fully cooked in the center, forcing me to either overcook the exterior or add more bread crumbs than I'd like so as to dry out the mixture. Just baking the burgers is fine, but in my opinion the absence of a crisp, "charred" exterior is far too much of a compromise. My method resolves this issue and offers the best of both worlds: a crispy exterior and fully cooked interior. It also facilitates a slightly wetter mixture—which means that fewer bread crumbs are needed—because the burgers will dry out a bit and firm up in the oven.

That said, sometimes the stovetop sear plus oven bake is a bit much for a weeknight, and there are other ways to cook them that also work well.

✳ **TO PANFRY:** Heat oil in a skillet—your widest one, if cooking multiple burgers at once (a 12-inch/30 cm skillet is ideal—over medium-high heat. When hot, add the burgers, as many as will fit comfortably in a single layer. Let sizzle for about a minute and then turn the heat to medium-low. Cook for 5 to 7 minutes, until evenly browned, then flip and finish cooking on the other side. They should feel slightly firm to the touch, and they will firm up further as they cool.

✳ **THE "SMASH BURGER" APPROACH:** This is a great method for vegan, bean-based burgers that may seem a touch too wet, such as the Chipotle Black Bean Burgers (page 92), or even the Spinach-Chickpea Burgers (page 81). Portion the veggie mixture into fat disks of about ⅓ cup (60 g) batter each. Heat your skillet over medium-high heat, add oil, then the burgers, allowing plenty of room between each one. Use a metal spatula to flatten the mounds to a thickness of ½ to ¾ inch (1.25–2 cm). Cook until well browned, usually 4 to 6 minutes, then flip and repeat. Thinner burgers like this have a higher proportion of crispy exterior, which provides helpful structural assistance.

✳ **TO BAKE:** This is a good method for burgers that are too delicate for the frying pan, such as Baked Cauliflower Burgers (page 74) and Baked Falafel Burgers (page 44). Preheat the oven to 375°F (190°C). Lightly grease a baking sheet, roasting pan, or other oven-safe pan. Transfer the burgers. Place in the oven and bake for 20 to 25 minutes, flipping halfway through, until firmed and lightly browned on each side.

✳ **TO GRILL:** Just about everyone likes food that's been prepared on an outdoor grill or barbecue, but that can be a challenge with homemade veggie burgers because so often they need to be cooked before they become firm enough to stay put over the grates of a grill. For best results, I typically precook my veggie burgers and then reheat them over the grill. But you can also treat the grill as more of an oven, cooking them in a heat-safe skillet or on a double layer of heavy-duty aluminum foil over indirect heat and with the lid closed. The burgers will require about 15 minutes of cooking time in a grill that's in the moderate heat range. Flip them halfway through. The strength of any grill's heat varies greatly, so be sure to keep an eye on the burgers. Watch for them to brown on the exterior and firm up, indicating that they are fully cooked through. If you want grill marks, place them directly over the grates once they've firmed up.

✳ **COOKING "SLIDERS":** Sauté the sliders in oil, turning once, for 6 to 10 minutes. It is not necessary to transfer them to the oven to finish heating. To keep a batch of sliders warm, preheat the oven to 275°F (140°C), line a baking sheet with parchment paper, transfer the sliders, and place in the oven. I often enjoy them when they're fully cooled; they make great snacks for packed lunches and road trips this way.

A NOTE ON OIL: Unless otherwise specified in these recipes, I recommend using an oil that is mild in flavor, is as minimally processed as possible, and that has a decent smoke point. I call for olive oil throughout the book, but feel free to substitute another oil, like avocado, grapeseed, or vegetable oil, if you prefer.

Leftovers

One thing I learned in developing my Made by Lukas veggie burger business is that the prepared veggie burger mix is a versatile ingredient on its own—you can do more with it than just shape it into burgers. Make sliders, or crumble it up into a hot pan and treat it like a veggie taco meat, or pack it into a mini loaf pan; or, if you or someone you're cooking for is an omnivore, you can use half veggie burger mix and half another ground protein to make burgers or loaves.

When I'm cooking for just one or two, I'll portion out just a few burgers, then pack up the leftover mix in a Tupperware for future burgers. I can cook them up later in whatever form I please.

Most of the burgers, uncooked or cooked, will keep for 3 to 5 days in the refrigerator. Uncooked burgers will keep for up to 2 months in the freezer. A whiff is usually enough to determine if they're still good to eat, but especially if they've been in the refrigerator a few days (and perhaps not stored under optimal conditions—see below), you may want to taste a little bit of a refrigerated burger before proceeding to cook the whole thing.

To freeze uncooked veggie burgers, pack the cooled leftover mixture into a freezer-safe Tupperware or place in an airtight container or resealable plastic bag. Uncooked veggie burger mix will freeze relatively well, but it will become significantly wetter when thawed. Allow time for it to thaw completely before cooking (leave it in the refrigerator overnight) and then blot dry with paper towels. If the mixture still seems too wet, fold in a few teaspoons of bread crumbs. Then shape as you please.

Leftover cooked burgers can be reheated on a lightly greased or parchment-lined baking sheet in a 300°F (150°C) oven for about 15 minutes. I also enjoy eating them cold or at room temperature, as a filling for a sandwich. I don't recommend freezing cooked veggie burgers, as the additional moisture that comes with freezing them makes the texture mushy.

Bean and Grain Burgers

Beans are arguably the ultimate veggie burger ingredient. They're a good source of protein (as well as fiber and other nutrients) for vegetarians and vegans, are inexpensive, will keep for months in your cupboards with minimal fuss, and—most importantly—are an expansive culinary foundation. They play a crucial role in many of the veggie burgers in this book, giving them their primary flavor and enhancing their overall structure.

The following are the beans used most in this cookbook.

❋ **BLACK BEANS:** Black beans have shiny black skins and a velvety interior. They are a staple of many cuisines and are famously good in veggie burgers, particularly because they're wonderfully starchy, meaning you can mash them up and the starches that are released can help bind the burgers.

❋ **CHICKPEAS:** The foundation for hummus, chickpeas are higher in protein than some other beans and have an unmistakable "eggy" taste. Chickpeas are a bit more vegetal and less starchy than black or red beans, so their binding properties aren't as good in veggie burgers. But their flavor is excellent, and they still break down nicely to provide wonderful body.

❋ **EDAMAME:** Edamame are simply young, fresh soybeans that were frozen rather than dried. They cook in a pot of salted water for about 3 minutes, and their tender, vegetal flavor and bright green color are entirely preserved. They don't have a lot of starch, so they can't be relied upon for any binding properties.

❋ **KIDNEY BEANS:** Red kidney beans have a mild flavor and are large and starchy, and, even more so than black beans, they make an excellent binder in place of eggs for vegan veggie burgers. White kidney beans are similar in texture and flavor and can be used interchangeably with navy, cannellini, and great northern beans (see below).

❋ **LENTILS:** There are over fifty different types of lentils available worldwide and they come in a rainbow of colors, but the three most commonly available are brown, red, and green lentils. Red lentils are split and thus have shorter cooking time; they will disintegrate after cooking—which, in some veggie burger recipes, is exactly what you want. French green lentils are known for holding their shape well in salads and other treatments, but that's not as helpful when you're trying to manipulate them into becoming a burger.

❋ **NAVY, CANNELLINI, AND GREAT NORTHERN BEANS:** These three are often grouped together, and they're all similar enough to be interchangeable in the recipes here. They're also starchy but have a light firmness and density. They're my favorite bean, and I love them in veggie burgers.

For bean cooking times and guidelines, see pages 12–13.

Easy Bean Burgers

Makes four 4-inch (10 cm) burgers

These simple burgers can be made from almost any medium or large bean, but the starchier ones work best: white beans, black beans, kidney beans. In those categories, I find that this recipe is also a good place to experiment with heirloom beans or a bean variety—particularly if you're multiplying the recipe to cook for a crowd. To make these vegan, simply omit the egg and substitute nutritional yeast for the cheese, then cook them "Smash Burger" style, as detailed on pages 23-24.

1½ cups (255 g) cooked beans

1 egg, beaten (optional; see headnote)

½ cup (30 g) roughly chopped fresh parsley

¼ cup (20 g) grated Parmesan or nutritional yeast

2 teaspoons Dijon mustard

½ teaspoon salt

¼ teaspoon freshly ground black pepper

Squeeze of fresh lemon juice

⅓ cup (20 g) panko or coarse bread crumbs, plus more if needed

2 tablespoons olive oil

1. In a mixing bowl, mash the beans using a potato masher or fork. Fold in the egg, if using, the parsley, Parmesan, mustard, salt, pepper, and lemon juice. Mix in the panko, adding more if the mixture is struggling to become malleable. Let stand for 5 to 10 minutes, so the panko soaks up some moisture. Adjust seasonings. Shape into 4 patties, about ⅓ cup (60 g) each.

2. To cook (see pages 23–24 for detailed cooking instructions), warm a wide skillet over medium heat, then add the oil. Add as many burgers as will fit comfortably without crowding the pan (usually 3 burgers will fit into a 10-inch/25 cm skillet), and cook until browned and crisped on the bottom, 5 to 7 minutes, then flip and repeat on the other side. The burgers will firm up a bit as they cook, and further once they're removed from the heat and have cooled slightly. Serve warm.

Spiced Lentil Burgers

Makes four 4-inch (10 cm) burgers

The inspiration for this burger came from Ani Chamichian, a friend whose family hails from Armenia and who introduced me to some of the primary flavors of the cuisine. The warm spices—doubly enforced by using whole spices as aromatics with the lentils, then added again to the veggie burger mixture—beautifully complement the earthy lentils. It's particularly good with Cucumber Yogurt Sauce (page 163). To veganize this recipe, I recommend using a steamed potato and potato starch, as detailed on page 18.

LENTILS

¾ cup (150 g) brown or green lentils

½ onion, cut into two quarters through the stem

2 whole cloves

1 teaspoon olive oil

1-inch (2.5 cm) piece ginger, cut into two pieces

2 garlic cloves, crushed and peeled

1 cinnamon stick

1 bay leaf

BURGERS

4 tablespoons olive oil

1 onion, diced

1¾ teaspoons ground allspice

½ teaspoon ground cinnamon

¼ teaspoon ground cloves

Pinch of cayenne pepper

3 garlic cloves, minced

2 teaspoons grated fresh ginger

1 egg, lightly beaten (optional; see headnote)

⅓ cup (20 g) panko or coarse bread crumbs, plus more if needed

⅓ cup (20 g) roughly chopped fresh parsley

½ teaspoon salt

Squeeze of fresh lemon juice

1. To cook the lentils, pick through the lentils and rinse thoroughly. Stud each onion quarter with a clove. Heat the oil in a medium saucepan over medium heat. Add the onion and the ginger, garlic, cinnamon stick, and bay leaf. Stir, then cover and cook for 1 minute, until fragrant. Add the lentils and 1½ cups (360 ml) water and bring to a boil. Reduce the heat, cover, and simmer for 15 to 20 minutes, until the lentils are tender. Compost the onion, ginger, garlic, cinnamon stick, and bay leaf, and pour off any excess liquid.

2. Heat 2 tablespoons of the oil in a sauté pan over medium-low heat. Add the onion, allspice, cinnamon, cloves, and cayenne. Cook, stirring frequently, until the onion begins to caramelize, about 10 to 12 minutes. Reduce the heat and add the garlic and ginger. Cook until the onion is fully cooked, about 5 minutes longer.

3. Set aside ½ cup (105 g) of the cooked lentils. In a food processor, combine the remaining lentils and the onion mixture with the egg, if using, and pulse until thoroughly combined. (You can also do this with a blender, pulsing as you go, or handheld immersion blender, which requires some patience.) Transfer to a mixing bowl. Add the reserved lentils and the panko, parsley, salt, and lemon juice. Adjust seasonings. Shape the mixture into patties, about ⅓ cup (60 g) each.

4. To cook (see pages 23–24 for detailed cooking instructions), warm a wide skillet over medium heat, then add the remaining oil. Add as many burgers as will fit comfortably without crowding the pan (usually 3 burgers will fit into a 10-inch/25 cm skillet), and cook until browned and crisped on the bottom, 5 to 7 minutes, then flip and repeat on the other side. The burgers will firm up a bit as they cook, and further once they're removed from the heat and have cooled slightly. Serve warm.

DO AHEAD: Cook lentils

SPICE TIPS

If you can find a spice shop that sells whole spices in bulk (as opposed to the packaged jars at the supermarket), you'll likely enjoy better flavor and definitely enjoy better savings. I find these to be most common at co-ops and health food stores, ones that sell loose-leaf teas in the same section of the market. Assuming there's plenty of turnover, the spices will be fresher, and you will be able to buy small amounts based on just what you need, often spending less than a dollar.

Furthermore, the flavor really is better when you buy spices whole and grind them yourself, either with a mortar and pestle or an electric spice grinder. In my experience, the trick to using a mortar and pestle for grinding spices is to be gentle, rather than forceful, tap-tap-tapping the spices until they crack open and begin to pulverize, rather than putting the force of your whole body into it, which gets tiring very quickly.

Lastly, when you have the time, toast your spices, too! Simply spread them out in a small, dry skillet over low heat until intoxicatingly fragrant. Allow them to cool before grinding (but transfer them to a plate or mortar—the residual heat in the skillet can cause them to burn). This applies even to black pepper. Try toasting the peppercorns before you fill your pepper mill and grind fresh over a dish.

Seeded Edamame Burgers with Brown Rice and Apples Ⓥ ㉓

Makes six 6-inch (15 cm) burgers

Here's a burger that may sound strange, given that it's studded with sesame seeds, sunflower seeds, and apple, and seasoned with soy sauce. But it's unexpectedly delicious, and its inspiration is a salad I regularly make that utilizes this same assortment of ingredients. It's sweet, savory, and refreshing. I sometimes like to use the "Smash Burger" cooking method on this burger, and it's essential that you give them a good sear on high heat when you first cook them. This searing—as well as the molasses—helps form the crust, which in turn holds the burgers together.

2 tablespoons hulled raw sunflower seeds

1 tablespoon raw sesame seeds

1 cup (115 g) frozen shelled edamame

2½ tablespoons ground flaxseed or flax meal (from 1 tablespoon whole seeds)

1½ cups (300 g) cooked brown rice (see page 15 for cooking instructions)

1 apple, peeled, cored, and coarsely grated or finely chopped

2 teaspoons cornstarch, potato starch, or arrowroot powder

1 teaspoons molasses

2 teaspoons soy sauce or tamari (GF)

1 teaspoon toasted sesame oil

A few grinds of black pepper

2 tablespoons olive oil

1. Toast the sunflower seeds in a dry skillet over medium-low heat until lightly browned and fragrant, about 5 minutes, swirling the pan periodically. Transfer to a heat-safe plate. In the same pan, toast the sesame seeds until golden brown and fragrant, swirling or stirring constantly to avoid overcooking and uneven browning. Transfer to the plate with the sunflower seeds.

2. Meanwhile, bring a saucepan of water to boil, and season it generously with salt. Add the edamame and cook for about 3 minutes (or according to package directions), until tender. Strain and rinse under cold water.

3. Whisk together the flaxseed and 3 tablespoons water. Let stand for about 5 minutes, until thickened.

4. In the bowl of a food processor, combine the toasted seeds, the edamame, and the flaxseed mixture with the rice, apple, cornstarch, molasses, soy sauce, sesame oil, and pepper. (If you don't have a food processor, you can finely grind the seeds with a mortar and pestle or spice mill and thoroughly mash the edamame by hand, then combine with the remining ingredients; if going this route, grate the apple rather than dice it.) Shape into 6 portions, about ⅓ cup (60 g) each.

5. To cook (see pages 23–24 for detailed cooking instructions), warm a wide skillet over medium heat, then add the oil. Add as many burgers as will fit comfortably without crowding the pan (usually 3 burgers will fit into a 10-inch/25 cm skillet), allowing plenty of space between. Use a metal spatula to flatten them out to a thickness of about ½ inch (1.25 cm), and cook until browned and crisped on the bottom, 5 to 7 minutes, then flip and repeat on the other side. The burgers will firm up a bit as they cook, and further once they're removed from the heat and have cooled slightly. Serve warm.

DO AHEAD: Toast seeds, cook edamame

MAKING USE OF LEFTOVER FRESH HERBS

In an ideal world, I would have an herb garden just outside the kitchen window and could pluck two sage leaves or a single sprig of thyme whenever the culinary inspiration strikes. But until that happens, I'll continue purchasing them from the farmers market and grocery store, where I inevitably must buy more of any one fresh herb than I need. Here are a few things I've learned to do with leftover herbs.

Proper Storage

First things first, when your herbs are stored properly, they can last over a week. Here's how to do it.

* Wash and dry thoroughly, using a salad spinner, then blot dry with a clean paper or kitchen towel.
* Spread the herbs out on a clean paper or kitchen towel. Then roll up into a loose cigar.
* Transfer this bundle to an airtight container.

Using More Herbs in Cooking

I think fresh herbs are more interchangeable than lots of recipes let on, and you can discover new flavor pairings that you like by taking a more freewheeling approach as you cook. Tender leafy herbs like parsley, cilantro, mint, basil, and dill are ones that I often mix and match, and I do the same with woodsy ones like thyme, rosemary, sage, and oregano, which are usually used in smaller quantities. They're all very different, of course, but often the purpose of the herb is to offer a jolt of distinctive freshness; its exact form of distinction can be variable.

As for tender herbs, think of them as a cousin of lettuces, and I incorporate the whole leaves into my salads by the handful.

Drying Herbs

Many years ago I took a cooking class in Paris. When the instructor, Paule Caillat, brought out a bunch of fresh thyme, one of my classmates asked whether she recommended cooking with fresh or dried herbs. Standing erect, Paule raised her wooden spoon in the air and waved it around: "This *herbs* business, I don't understand. You start with the herbs fresh, and over time the herbs become dry. Non?" Since then, I've been drying most of my leftover fresh herbs.

There are several methods, but here are three that work best for me.

❋ **TIED AND HUNG:** Tie up the herbs at the stem with kitchen twine. Pierce a small paper bag a few times with a small knife or skewer. Place the bag over the herbs, holding them upright, and close the bag around the stems, tying it with string or kitchen twine. Hang the bag from the stems in a place where it will be out of the way—the corner of a closet or cupboard works best for me—and let hang for a week or two, until the herbs are fully dried. Crunch up the leaves while still inside the bag—the idea behind the bag is that it collects herbs as they dry and fall, and protects them from dust and other particles in the air—and then pour out the dried leaves, composting the stems. Store in a small, airtight container.

❋ **SLOW DRYING METHOD:** Remove the fresh herb leaves from their stems and mince. Spread out the leaves between layers of dry paper or kitchen towels. Let these stand for 5 to 8 days, until fully dried. Store in a small, airtight container.

❋ **FAST OVEN-DRYING METHOD:** Preheat the oven to 300°F (150°C). Line a baking sheet with parchment paper, then set a cooling rack on top of it. Arrange the herbs over the cooling rack, spacing them out in an even layer. Transfer to the oven and turn it off. Leave the herbs there for 2 hours or up to overnight, until they're curled, completely dry, and crisp. If they aren't fully dried out when you first check on them, simply leave them in the oven longer. You can speed things along by applying more heat, but if you do, remove the tray while the oven preheats, then repeat as before. To separate the leaves from the stems, carefully lift the cooling rack off the parchment and, working stem by stem, gently swipe or crumble the leaves onto the parchment paper. They should come off easily, leaving the stems clean.

Tuscan White Bean Burgers

Makes four 4-inch (10 cm) burgers

This is inspired by one of my favorite simple ways to enjoy creamy white beans, which is around a flavor profile of sweet roasted garlic and a woody herb like rosemary or thyme. I like to top the burgers with a handful of parsley or arugula, olives, and a squeeze of lemon juice, as pictured. All the burgers in this book can be served off the bun, over salad or as sliders, but this one is particularly good when given the salad format, since it complements the bracing pepperiness of greens like mature arugula so well.

1 head garlic

4 tablespoons plus ½ teaspoon olive oil

1 onion, peeled and sliced into thin rings

1½ cups (255 g) cooked white beans (cannellini or navy beans)

1 egg

3 fresh sage leaves, minced, or 1 teaspoon dried

½ cup (60 g) pitted Kalamata olives, sliced

Squeeze of fresh lemon juice

½ cup (30 g) panko or coarse bread crumbs, plus more if needed

Salt

Freshly ground black pepper

1. To roast the garlic, preheat the oven to 400°F (200°C). Slice the top ½-inch (1.25 cm) or so from the garlic head so that most of the cloves are exposed. Take two squares of aluminum foil and stack them on top of one another place the garlic in the center. Cup the foil around the garlic, then drizzle with the ½ teaspoon oil and add a splash of water. Seal up the garlic inside the foil and transfer to the oven. Cook until completely tender and golden, 30 to 45 minutes, or more if needed. Test by piercing a large clove with a skewer or paring knife; it should meet no resistance. Cool, then squeeze out all the garlic from the head into a small bowl. (You can roast several heads of garlic at a time using this method, arranging them in a small baking dish and sealing tightly with foil.)

2. Meanwhile, caramelize the onions. Heat 2 tablespoons of the remaining oil in a heavy-bottomed sauté pan over medium heat, then add the onion, turning to coat. Cover the pan and cook for 10 minutes, then uncover and continue cooking, stirring occasionally and lowering the heat if the onion begins to burn, until deeply golden and caramelized, another 20 to 30 minutes. Cool.

3. In a food processor, purée ½ cup (85 g) of the beans with half the roasted garlic, half the caramelized onion, the egg, and half the sage. (If you don't have a food processor, use a potato masher to thoroughly combine these ingredients in a mixing bowl, then proceed with the remaining step.)

4. Chop the remaining caramelized onion and roasted garlic coarsely and place in a mixing bowl. Add the remaining beans and coarsely mash with a potato masher.

Fold in the puréed bean-egg mixture, the remaining sage, the olives, and the lemon juice. Fold in the panko, adding more if necessary—just until the mixture begins to pull from the side of the bowl (it will be a wet mixture). Season with salt and pepper. Shape into 4 patties, about a heaping ⅓ cup (60 g) each.

5. To cook (see pages 23–24 for detailed cooking instructions), warm a wide skillet over medium heat, then add the remaining oil. Add as many burgers as will fit comfortably without crowding the pan (usually 3 burgers will fit into a 10-inch/25 cm skillet), and cook until browned and crisped on the bottom, 5 to 7 minutes, then flip and repeat on the other side. The burgers will firm up a bit as they cook, and further once they're removed from the heat and have cooled slightly. Serve warm.

DO AHEAD: Caramelize onions, roast garlic

Kale and Quinoa Burgers Ⓥ ⒼⒻ

Makes six 4-inch (10 cm) burgers

When I had my Made by Lukas veggie burger business, a lot of people liked the idea of a kale burger. But the reality of developing one that tastes good wasn't so simple. Kale is a bitter vegetable that needs fattiness as a counterpoint, and it also cooks down dramatically, meaning that you need a *lot* of kale to make it feel like you're actually eating a kale burger. It took a while to find the right solutions, one of them being to supplement the kale with cabbage, which has more body and develops sweetness when it cooks, to further soften the bitterness and to add a bit of richness with cashews.

¼ cup (45 g) quinoa, rinsed if not prerinsed

1 teaspoon salt

1 big bunch kale

4 tablespoons olive oil

1 medium onion, diced

2 cups (115 g) finely shredded cabbage

3 garlic cloves, minced

¼ teaspoon crushed red pepper flakes

Zest of 1 lemon plus juice of ½

⅓ cup (50 g) coarsely chopped, toasted cashews

2 tablespoons toasted sesame seeds

1 teaspoon cornstarch, potato starch, or arrowroot powder

¼ cup (15 g) potato flakes

1. In a small saucepan, combine the quinoa with ½ cup (120 ml) water. Bring to a boil, add ¼ teaspoon of the salt, then reduce the heat to low and cover the pan. Cook gently for 18 to 20 minutes, until the water is absorbed and the germ of the quinoa is exposed. Set aside uncovered, to cool as you prepare the remaining ingredients.

2. Separate the kale stems from the leaves, then coarsely chop the leaves. You can finely chop the stems and include them in the burgers, though they do add some fibrous texture—if you wish to include the stems, be diligent about chopping them finely; otherwise, compost them.

3. Warm the olive oil in a wide skillet over medium heat. Add the onions and cook until softened and beginning to caramelize, 8 to 10 minutes. Stir in the kale, add the cabbage and the remaining salt, then cover and cook until completely tender, 7 to 10 minutes. If the pan seems too dry, add a splash of water. Uncover, stir in the garlic and red pepper flakes and cook for another minute, until fragrant. Remove from the heat and set aside to cool slightly.

4. In the bowl of a food processor, combine the cashews, sesame seeds, cornstarch, and the cabbage-kale mixture. Pulse several times, until the seeds are well ground and the vegetables finely chopped. Add the quinoa and the potato flakes and pulse a few times more, to just combine. The mixture should be just moist enough to easily shape into burgers. If too dry, pulse in 1 to 2 tablespoons water. Shape into 6 burgers.

5. To cook (see pages 23–24 for detailed cooking instructions), warm a wide skillet over medium heat, then add the remaining oil. Add as many burgers as will fit comfortably without crowding the pan (usually 3 burgers will fit into a 10-inch/25 cm skillet), and cook until browned and crisped on the bottom, 5 to 7 minutes, then flip and repeat on the other side. The burgers will firm up a bit as they cook, and further once they're removed from the heat and have cooled slightly. Serve warm.

Baked Falafel Burgers Ⓥ ⒼⒻ

Makes four 4-inch (10 cm) burgers

In this falafel method, the chickpeas are soaked overnight but not cooked. (If we were deep-frying the burgers rather than baking them, this would be the traditional falafel method.) Store-bought falafel mixes—many of which are wonderful—use ground, unsoaked dried beans, but I find that the soaking makes for a significantly less dense, more tender falafel. The mixture is a bit more delicate than other burgers in this book, but you'll be amazed at how vibrant the flavors are, how the parsley and lemon shine through. Serve with Cucumber Yogurt Sauce (page 163), Tahini Yogurt Sauce (page 163), or plain tahini along with a squirt of sriracha, as a nod to the street food that fed me throughout my college years. Unfortunately, cooked chickpeas will not work in this recipe; there will be too much liquid and the burgers will fall apart as they cook.

1 cup (190 g) dried chickpeas, rinsed thoroughly

1 onion, roughly chopped

2 garlic cloves

½ cup (30 g) roughly chopped fresh parsley

Zest of 1 lemon plus juice of ½

1 tablespoon toasted cumin seeds

½ teaspoon baking soda (GF)

¾ teaspoon salt

½ teaspoon freshly ground black pepper

¼ teaspoon cayenne pepper

1 tablespoon chickpea or all-purpose flour, if needed

Olive oil, for greasing

1. Cover the chickpeas with 4 to 5 inches (10–13 cm) of water in a bowl and let stand for 24 hours. Drain thoroughly.

2. Preheat the oven to 400°F (200°C).

3. Combine the chickpeas, onion, garlic, parsley, lemon zest and juice, cumin, baking soda, salt, pepper, and cayenne in a food processor. Pulse until coarsely combined. If the mixture is struggling to come together, add a bit of water, but no more than 2 tablespoons. (The burgers will fall apart when cooking if there's too much liquid.) If water is added, stir in the chickpea flour. Adjust seasonings. Shape into 6 patties, about ⅓ cup (60 g) each. It will be a fairly wet dough.

4. Liberally oil a baking sheet. Transfer the patties to the baking sheet and place in the oven. Bake for 15 to 20 minutes, flipping them once halfway through, until golden and firm. Serve warm.

Cashew-Leek Burgers
with Bulgur and Lentils

Makes six 4-inch (10 cm) burgers

This burger takes its inspiration from America's Test Kitchen's original veggie burger, which piqued my interest because of its pairing of lentils, bulgur, and cashews. Bulgur can be such an incredibly valuable grain to keep around, because it's so easy to cook—just cover with boiling water and let stand to rehydrate. Using their flavor profile as a guide, I put caramelized leeks and roasted cashews at the fore, because the sweetness of the two is a wonderful pairing. Also, whole wheat bread crumbs bring a wonderful toastiness (you can use panko or other bread crumbs as well—but whole wheat is really nice here).

⅓ cup (66 g) brown lentils

⅓ cup (50 g) bulgur

4 tablespoons olive oil, divided

8 cremini mushrooms, thinly sliced

2 medium leeks, cleaned and finely chopped (see page 48)

½ teaspoon dried thyme

2 garlic cloves, minced

1 tablespoon tomato paste

½ cup (75 g) toasted cashews

2 eggs

1 teaspoon salt

¼ teaspoon freshly ground black pepper

1 cup (60 g) coarse whole wheat bread crumbs, or panko or other coarse bread crumbs

1. To cook the lentils, pick through the lentils and rinse thoroughly. Bring the lentils and at least 2 cups (480 ml) water to a boil in a small saucepan. Cover, reduce the heat, and simmer for 20 to 25 minutes, until the lentils are cooked and beginning to fall apart. Strain, then transfer to a baking sheet or mixing bowl to cool.

2. Meanwhile, bring ⅔ cup (160 ml) water to a boil. Stir in the bulgur with a pinch of salt, cover, and remove from the heat. Let stand for about 7 minutes, until all the liquid is absorbed.

3. Heat 1 tablespoon of the oil in a sauté pan over medium heat. Add the mushrooms and cook until they release their liquid and it cooks off, 8 to 10 minutes. Transfer to a large mixing bowl and wipe out the pan.

4. Heat 1 tablespoon of the remaining oil in the sauté pan over medium heat. Add the leeks and thyme and cook, stirring frequently, until the leeks are completely softened and beginning to caramelize, 15 to 20 minutes. Stir in the garlic and tomato paste and cook for 2 minutes longer. Transfer to the bowl with the mushrooms and stir to mix.

5. In the bowl of a food processor, combine half the lentils, half the bulgur, and half the leek mixture with the cashews, eggs, salt, and pepper. Pulse until uniformly puréed but still slightly chunky. Add the remaining lentils and bulgur and pulse, to just mix together, followed by the bread crumbs. Shape the mixture into 6 patties, about ⅓ cup (60 g) each.

6. To cook (see pages 23–24 for detailed cooking instructions), warm a wide skillet over medium heat, then, add the remaining oil. Add as many burgers as will fit comfortably without crowding the pan (usually 3 burgers will fit into a 10-inch/25 cm skillet), and cook until browned and crisped on the bottom, 5 to 7 minutes, then flip and repeat on the other side. The burgers will firm up a bit as they cook, and further once they're removed from the heat and have cooled slightly. Serve warm.

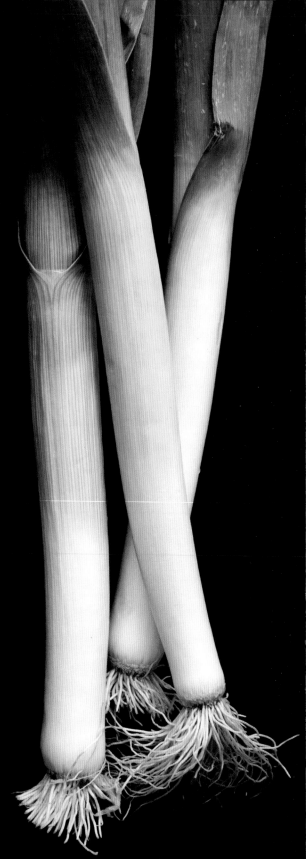

HOW TO CLEAN LEEKS

Leeks are notorious for having bits of sand and dirt lodged throughout, and there are many ways to clean them. One popular method is to slice off the roots and then quarter the leeks lengthwise from the root end to a few inches into the dark green parts (the leek is still in one piece, connected from the top). Pull the leeks open, blossom-like, and gently rub their insides under running water to rid them of dirt.

Or you can chop them before cleaning, cover them with cold water in a large bowl, and swish them around with your hands to dislodge the dirt. Change the water and repeat. Drain in a sieve or colander.

Fava Bean Burgers

Makes six 4-inch (10 cm) burgers

This burger calls for dried or canned fava beans (also known as broad beans) rather than fresh ones. Dried and reconstituted favas don't have the vibrant green color of their fresh counterparts, but the flavor is familiarly ripe and slightly sour, if you know what the fresh ones taste like, and here they're balanced out with chickpeas and then finished with a medley of fresh herbs. Health food stores carry dried favas (you can save yourself some time by buying them pre-shelled), but to find canned, you'll probably need to hunt them down at a specialty grocery or Middle Eastern grocery.

3 tablespoons olive oil

1 onion, diced

1½ cups (255 g) cooked fava beans (see headnote)

1 cup (170 g) cooked chickpeas

½ cup (50 g) toasted walnuts, coarsely chopped

2 eggs, beaten

2 tablespoons chopped fresh chives

2 tablespoons chopped fresh parsley

2 tablespoons coarsely chopped fresh basil

¾ teaspoon salt

¼ teaspoon freshly ground black pepper

1½ cups (90 g) panko or coarse bread crumbs

1. Preheat the oven to 375°F (190°C).

2. Heat 1 tablespoon of the oil in a sauté pan over medium heat. Add the onion and cook until translucent, 8 to 10 minutes.

3. In the bowl of a food processor, combine the onion with the fava beans, chickpeas, and walnuts. Process until coarsely combined. Add the eggs, chives, parsley, basil, salt, and pepper, pulsing to further combine. Add the panko and pulse a few times, until just combined. Shape into 6 patties, about ⅓ cup (60 g) each. Let stand for 20 minutes.

4. To cook (see pages 23–24 for detailed cooking instructions), warm a wide skillet over medium heat, then add the remaining oil. Add as many burgers as will fit comfortably without crowding the pan (usually 3 burgers will fit into a 10-inch/25 cm skillet), and cook until browned and crisped on the bottom, 5 to 7 minutes, then flip and repeat on the other side. The burgers will firm up a bit as they cook, and further once they're removed from the heat and have cooled slightly. Serve warm.

Quinoa, Red Bean, and Walnut Burgers Ⓥ ⒼⒻ

Makes six 4-inch (10 cm) burgers

This is an incredibly simple burger, and it's a perfect illustration of how potato can function so well as a binder, particularly when paired with starchy red beans. As with many other vegan burgers, this is one you don't even have to cook, but of course you'll want to, because cooking with the pomegranate sesame sauce creates a tart and nutty glaze on the burger that makes it very unique.

½ cup (90 g) quinoa, rinsed thoroughly

1 small potato, peeled and chopped into 1-inch (2.5 cm) pieces

3 tablespoons olive oil

1 bunch scallions, including an inch of the green parts, thinly sliced

½ cup (30 g) roughly chopped fresh parsley

2 tablespoons minced fresh ginger

1½ cups (255 g) cooked red beans

½ cup (50 g) toasted walnuts, finely chopped

½ teaspoon salt

Juice of ½ lemon

2 tablespoons Pomegranate-Sesame Sauce (page 158)

1. Combine the quinoa with 1 cup (240 ml) water in a small saucepan and bring to a boil. Reduce to a simmer, cover, and cook for 15 minutes, until the water is absorbed. Let stand for 5 minutes.

2. Meanwhile, steam or boil the potato until tender. Mash with a fork.

3. Heat 1 tablespoon of the oil in a medium skillet over medium heat. Add the scallions and cook just until fragrant, 1 to 2 minutes. Add the parsley and ginger and cook until fragrant, about 30 seconds.

4. In a large bowl, combine the quinoa, potato, parsley-scallion mixture, and the red beans and walnuts with a potato masher or with your hands. Add the salt and lemon juice. Shape into 6 patties, about ⅓ cup (60 g) each.

5. To cook (see pages 23–24 for detailed cooking instructions), warm a wide skillet over medium heat, then add the remaining oil. Add as many burgers as will fit comfortably without crowding the pan (usually 3 burgers will fit into a 10-inch/25 cm skillet), and cook until browned and crisped on the bottom, 4 to 5 minutes. Drizzle a spoonful (about 1½ teaspoons per burger) of the pomegranate sauce over the burger, then flip and repeat on the other side, cooking it until browned. Serve warm.

Red Lentil and Celeriac Burgers Ⓥ

Makes six 4-inch (10 cm) burgers

Red lentils have a subtler, slightly sweeter flavor and much less structure when cooked than their brown and green cousins. In fact, they mostly turn to mush, are primarily common in soup-like treatments and dals, and don't really work in salads at all. But for a veggie burger, the mush can be useful. Here they're paired with celeriac, which offsets them with a lovely, clean finish and provides some body. Look for a celeriac that is firm; to prepare for cooking, use a sharp chef's knife to cut off all the dark brown exterior. These can be somewhat delicate burgers, and if you have the time to follow the sear-then-bake method outlined on page 23, they'll hold together best.

1 cup (200 g) red lentils

1 celeriac, peeled and cut into ½-inch (1.25 cm) dice

3 tablespoons olive oil

1 medium onion, diced

½ teaspoons dried thyme or 1 tablespoon fresh

¼ cup (60 ml) dry red wine

2 tablespoons roughly chopped fresh parsley

¾ teaspoon salt

½ teaspoon freshly ground black pepper

½ cup toasted bread crumbs, plus more if needed

1. Preheat the oven to 375°F (190°C).

2. To cook the lentils, pick through the lentils and rinse thoroughly. Combine the lentils and at least 2 cups (480 ml) water in a small saucepan and bring to a boil. Cover, reduce the heat, and simmer for 20 to 25 minutes, until the lentils are cooked and beginning to fall apart. Drain off any liquid left in the pan, and transfer to a baking sheet or mixing bowl to cool.

3. Meanwhile, in a medium saucepan or pot, cover the celeriac with cold water. Bring to a boil over high heat and generously season with salt. Reduce the heat and simmer until the celeriac is fork-tender, 10 to 15 minutes. Drain and place in the bowl of a food processor with half the lentils. Pulse until combined but still slightly chunky.

4. Wipe out the pan and heat 1 tablespoon of the oil over medium heat. Add the onion. If using dried thyme instead of fresh, add it now. Sauté until the onion is lightly browned, 10 to 12 minutes. If using fresh thyme, add it now and stir for 30 seconds, until fragrant. Deglaze the pan with the red wine and cook until most of the liquid has evaporated, about 2 minutes.

5. Add the onions and the parsley, salt, pepper, and the remaining lentils to the food processor, and pulse until just combined. Add the bread crumbs, pulsing to combine. If the mixture seems too wet, add additional bread crumbs by the tablespoon. Let stand for 10 minutes. Shape into 6 patties.

6. To cook (see pages 23–24 for detailed cooking instructions), warm a wide oven-safe skillet over medium-high heat, then add a splash of oil. Add as many burgers as will fit comfortably without crowding the pan (usually 3 burgers will fit into a 10-inch/25 cm skillet), and cook until browned on each side, 6 to 10 minutes. Transfer the pan to the oven and bake for 12 to 15 minutes. The burgers will firm up a bit as they cook, and further once they're removed from the heat and have cooled slightly. Serve warm.

Baked Quinoa Burgers

Makes six 4-inch (10 cm) burgers

These are super simple burgers that have a lot in common with little grain cakes or fritters, in that the main principle here is quinoa bound together with egg. By baking, the quinoa dries out and gives these burgers a crunchy crust that I love, and because the grain cooks so quickly, they can be ready to go in the time it takes for the oven to preheat. Take your pick between the pepper flakes or nutmeg depending on whether you'd like a touch of heat or a slightly floral note. I rarely make it to condiments with these, opting instead to eat them completely unadorned, and they work great as two- or three-bite sliders in this way.

1 cup (180 g) quinoa

5 ounces (150 g) spinach, fresh or frozen

1 small shallot, minced

2 garlic cloves, minced

1 egg, beaten

3 tablespoons all-purpose flour or gluten-free flour blend

1 teaspoon baking powder

1 teaspoon sea salt

¼ teaspoon freshly ground black pepper

Pinch red pepper flakes or freshly grated nutmeg

1. Preheat the oven to 400°F (200°C). Line a baking sheet with parchment paper.

2. Thoroughly rinse and drain the quinoa. Combine the quinoa with 1¾ cups (420 ml) water in a small saucepan and bring to a boil. Reduce the heat and add a pinch of salt. Cover and simmer for 10 to 15 minutes, until the water is absorbed. Transfer to a mixing bowl and allow to cool slightly.

3. Meanwhile, prepare the spinach. If using fresh spinach, steam it for 3 to 4 minutes over an inch of simmering water using a collapsible steamer basket, or blanch it for 30 seconds in a pot of boiling salted water. Transfer to an ice bath to halt the cooking. Squeeze dry and finely chop. If using frozen spinach, allow it to thaw and then squeeze dry.

4. Combine the quinoa and the spinach with the shallot, garlic, egg, flour, baking powder, salt, pepper, and red pepper flakes in a mixing bowl. Shape into 6 patties and arrange on the prepared baking sheet.

5. Bake for 15 to 20 minutes, rotating the baking sheet halfway through, until golden brown and firm. Serve warm.

Pub Grub Veggie Burgers

Makes eight 4-inch (10 cm) burgers

I've had many veggie burgers at pubs and restaurants that taste just a little bit too good. *What's the secret?* I'd wonder. When I probed the server at one restaurant for what exactly made their offering so good, what she told me—a combination of beans, cheese, and chili powder—didn't seem to completely add up. I finally figured out the secret of the pub veggie burger: Like most everything else on the menu, it was deep-fried. (I ultimately landed on shallow-frying for this recipe, which makes more sense at home. But if you want to fully deep-fry, see page 141 for a few guidelines.) The addition of a melty cheese also ups the pub grub factor, too.

1 onion, chopped

3 eggs

1½ cups (255 g) cooked black beans

1½ cups (255 g) cooked chickpeas

1 teaspoon chili powder

1 teaspoon salt

1½ cups (90 g) panko

1 cup (115 g) grated melting cheese such as pepper jack, Muenster, mozzarella, or Fontina cheese

¼ cup (115 g) chopped fresh parsley

Peanut, canola, or vegetable oil, for shallow-frying

1. In the bowl of a food processor, combine the onion, eggs, beans, chickpeas, chili powder, and salt. Pulse until combined but still slightly chunky. Add the panko, cheese, and parsley, and pulse a few times more. Shape into 8 patties.

2. Heat ½ inch (1.25 cm) oil in a deep skillet or sauté pan over medium-high heat. Cook the patties in batches to avoid crowding, turning once, until uniformly browned, 8 to 12 minutes. Line a plate with paper towels or flattened paper bags. Transfer the burgers to drain of excess oil. Serve warm.

Vegetable Burgers

This is what it's all about, isn't it?

A veggie burger is nothing if not a celebration of vegetables, and these recipes are a pride parade of what's typically relegated to the perimeters of Hamburger Nation. I have yet to encounter a vegetable that has disappointed me in a veggie burger, even though I sometimes have had to finesse certain vegetables with additional ingredients in order to bring them to their full potential.

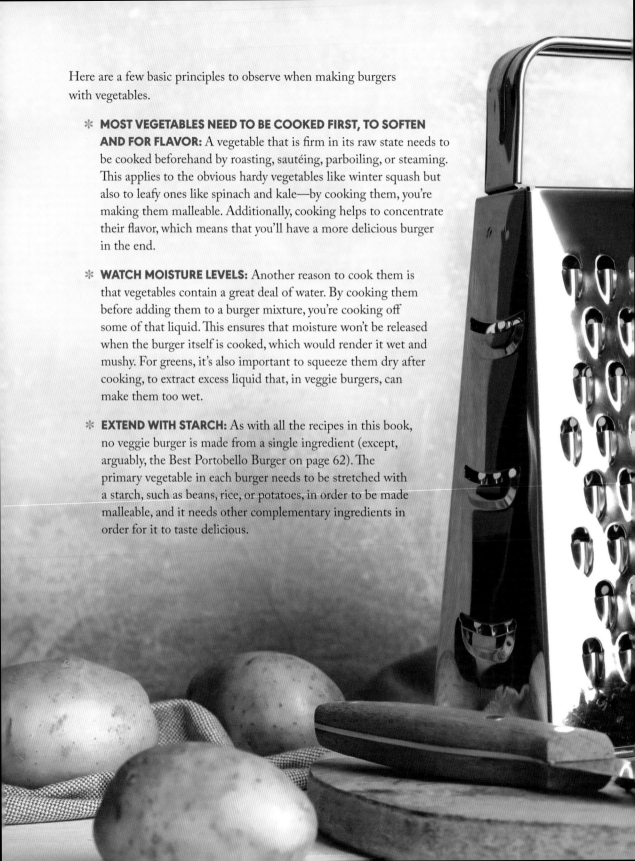

Here are a few basic principles to observe when making burgers with vegetables.

✳ **MOST VEGETABLES NEED TO BE COOKED FIRST, TO SOFTEN AND FOR FLAVOR:** A vegetable that is firm in its raw state needs to be cooked beforehand by roasting, sautéing, parboiling, or steaming. This applies to the obvious hardy vegetables like winter squash but also to leafy ones like spinach and kale—by cooking them, you're making them malleable. Additionally, cooking helps to concentrate their flavor, which means that you'll have a more delicious burger in the end.

✳ **WATCH MOISTURE LEVELS:** Another reason to cook them is that vegetables contain a great deal of water. By cooking them before adding them to a burger mixture, you're cooking off some of that liquid. This ensures that moisture won't be released when the burger itself is cooked, which would render it wet and mushy. For greens, it's also important to squeeze them dry after cooking, to extract excess liquid that, in veggie burgers, can make them too wet.

✳ **EXTEND WITH STARCH:** As with all the recipes in this book, no veggie burger is made from a single ingredient (except, arguably, the Best Portobello Burger on page 62). The primary vegetable in each burger needs to be stretched with a starch, such as beans, rice, or potatoes, in order to be made malleable, and it needs other complementary ingredients in order for it to taste delicious.

＊ YOUR BOX GRATER IS YOUR FRIEND: Once I realized that tough root vegetables like beets and carrots—and even hardy winter squash and sweet potatoes—can be quickly prepped by coarsely grating them using a box grater (or the grater attachment of your food processor, if you prefer), it unlocked a world of new veggie burger ideas. This is a terrific method because, while yes, it does speed up prep and streamlines the cooking method by eliminating the need to pre-roast or otherwise precook your veg, it produces a texture that's perfect for veggie burgers. These veg become malleable but also retain some of their original texture. You'll find this method in several of the recipes that follow.

Sesame Sweet Potato and Cabbage Burgers

Makes four 4-inch (10 cm) burgers

This is a veggie burger I've always loved for its unexpected richness, thanks to the combination of sweet browned onions, sesame oil, and tahini. It's worthwhile to cook the onions with some care, so as to allow them to caramelize and become sweet. And any variety of sweet potato will work—the purple ones lending the most distinctive color. Serve with one of the yogurt sauces on pages 162–63, or simply drizzled with tahini and some crisp vegetables like cucumber slices, sprouts, or lettuce.

4 tablespoons olive oil

1 large or 2 small onions, chopped

Scant ¼ teaspoon cayenne pepper

1 tablespoon toasted sesame oil

1 medium sweet potato, coarsely grated

2 cups (178 g) finely shredded cabbage

1 teaspoon salt

1 egg

1 tablespoon tahini

Juice of 1 lemon

¼ cup (15 g) panko or coarse bread crumbs, plus more if needed

1. Heat 2 tablespoons of the oil in your widest skillet over medium-high heat. Add the onion and cayenne and fry until soft and beginning to color deeply, 10 to 12 minutes. Add the sesame oil, followed by the sweet potato, cabbage, and salt. Cover and cook until tender, stirring periodically, about 10 minutes. Allow to cool slightly.

2. Whisk together the egg, tahini, and lemon juice until combined. Add the potato-cabbage mixture, then fold in the panko. Add additional bread crumbs if the mixture seems loose, but err on the side of wet because the burgers will firm up in the oven. Shape into 4 patties.

3. To cook (see pages 23–24 for detailed cooking instructions), warm a wide skillet over medium heat, then add the remaining oil. Add as many burgers as will fit comfortably without crowding the pan (usually 3 burgers will fit into a 10-inch/25 cm skillet), and cook until browned and crisped on the bottom, 5 to 7 minutes, then flip and repeat on the other side. The burgers will firm up a bit as they cook, and further once they're removed from the heat and have cooled slightly. Serve warm.

Best Portobello Burgers Ⓥ ⒼⒻ

Makes four 4-inch (10 cm) burgers

No matter how many variations on a hamburger that a typical burger joint menu offers, the prevailing way of preparing portobello mushroom burgers—and the vegetarian portobello-as-meat default—at restaurants seems to be to drench them in cheap, cloyingly sweet balsamic vinegar marinade. The first thing I realized when I began developing my portobello burger was that the mushroom needed a savory marinade to double down on the mushroom's inherent umami characteristics. Enter miso paste! For years I've been adding it to salad dressings and marinades to lend savory depth that only a fermented food can achieve. No surprise, it works perfectly in a veggie burger like this one.

4 medium portobello mushrooms

3 tablespoons olive oil

1 tablespoon rice vinegar

1 tablespoon miso paste

½ teaspoon freshly ground black pepper

1. Trim or gently twist off the stems of the mushrooms, and scrape out the gills with a spoon. Place the caps in a large baking dish or mixing bowl.

2. In a small bowl, whisk together the oil, vinegar, miso, and pepper. Pour over the mushrooms and, using your hands, toss to ensure that all the mushrooms are evenly coated. Marinate for at least 15 minutes or up to 2 hours.

3. Heat a large sauté pan over medium-high heat. Add the mushrooms, rounded tops down, and cook for 10 to 15 minutes, flipping them halfway through, until cooked thoroughly. The mushrooms should be tender in the thick center—test with a small, sharp knife. You can also watch for them to release their liquid and for most of it to cook off. Serve warm.

Grill method: Prepare a medium fire over a charcoal or gas grill. Grill the mushrooms over an open flame for a total of 10 to 12 minutes, beginning with the rounded top down and flipping halfway through.

VARIATIONS

- Stuffed portobello burgers with cheese: Mash together 1 cup (200 g) cooked brown rice, ½ cup (85 g) red or black beans, and a generous pinch of salt. Spread this mixture over the undersides of the cooked mushrooms and then lay a slice of mozzarella, Monterey Jack, queso fresco, white cheddar, or your favorite vegan cheese over the mixture. Place under the broiler or on the grill, covered, for a few moments, until the cheese melts. Serve open-faced on a grilled slab of ciabatta or other airy bread.

- Spinach and cheese portobello burgers: Martha Rose Shulman of *The New York Times* recommends melting a slice of Gruyère cheese over the top of a cooked mushroom under the broiler or in the pan, fitting a small mound of blanched chopped spinach between the hamburger bun and the cavity of the mushroom. This is delicious on Whole Wheat Burger Buns (page 112).

- California portobello burgers: On a Basic Burger Bun (page 110), place a cooked mushroom over a layer of avocado slices and a few splashes of hot sauce or sriracha, then top with Quick-Pickled Red Onions (page 156) and a handful of sprouts or microgreens.

Beet and Brown Rice Burgers Ⓥ ⒼⒻ

Makes six 4-inch (10 cm) burgers

Red wine vinegar is a natural pair for beets, and this burger makes judicious use of it. "Searing" this delicate burger on high heat at the beginning of the cooking process is important—you'll want to follow the "Smash Burger" cooking method as outlined on pages 23-24. The crust that forms is what helps the burger keep its shape. It's also helpful to be thorough—and even use your hands—to mash up the beans, so as to make the most of their binding properties. I like to top this one with the Quick-Pickled Red Onions (page 156) and a handful of tender salad greens, and any of the yogurt sauces on pages 162-63 are also very good.

3 medium beets, scrubbed clean, ends trimmed

4 tablespoons olive oil

1 red onion, diced

½ teaspoon salt

1 tablespoon red wine vinegar

1½ cups (255 g) cooked black or red beans

½ cup (50 g) cooked brown rice

2 teaspoons cornstarch, potato starch, or arrowroot powder

2 tablespoons chopped fresh parsley

Freshly ground black pepper

1. Using the large holes of a box grater or the grater blade of your food processor, grate the beets. (It's not necessary to peel them first.)

2. Heat 2 tablespoons of the oil in a large, lidded sauté pan over medium heat. Add the onion and cook until it softens and begins to look translucent, 6 to 8 minutes. Add the beets and the salt and toss to combine. Cover and cook for 10 to 12 minutes, until the beets are completely softened. Add the vinegar, toss to combine, and keep cooking until the pan is dry. Use a wooden spoon to scrape up the browned bits from the pan. Set aside to cool slightly.

3. In a mixing bowl, coarsely mash the beans with a potato masher or fork. Fold in the beet mixture and the rice, cornstarch, and parsley, and season with pepper. Shape into 6 patties, flattening to a ½-inch (1.25 cm) thickness.

4. To cook (see pages 23–24 for detailed cooking instructions), warm a wide skillet over medium-high heat, then add the remaining oil. Add as many burgers as will fit comfortably without crowding the pan (usually 3 burgers will fit into a 10-inch/25 cm skillet), and use a metal spatula to flatten them slightly. Cook until browned and crisped on the bottom, 5 to 7 minutes, then flip and repeat on the other side. The burgers will firm up a bit as they cook, and further once they're removed from the heat and have cooled slightly. Serve warm.

Spicy Peanut and Carrot Burgers

Makes four 6-inch (15 cm) burgers

This recipe helped me realize that coarsely shredding hardy vegetables, like carrots, is the secret to creating a vegetable-centric veggie burger—it preserves more of a vegetable's texture than, say, roasting and puréeing it, and moreover it gives an interesting and varied texture to the finished burger. Peanut butter and a few fragrant aromatics serve to amplify and enhance the carrot, making this another one of those veggie burgers that's all about the vegetables. A natural peanut butter will deliver a clean peanut flavor, whereas a processed one that has added sugar will be kind of cloying here. I love these paired with a zesty cabbage slaw, either the one on page 127 or some shredded cabbage that's tossed with a bit of salt and lime juice.

3 tablespoons olive oil

4 scallions, green and white parts, thinly sliced

3 garlic cloves, minced

1 tablespoon finely grated fresh ginger

1 serrano chile pepper, finely chopped (and seeded, if desired)

4 cups (360 g) grated carrots (about 8 medium carrots)

1 teaspoon salt

1 teaspoon ground coriander

¾ teaspoon ground turmeric

½ teaspoon ground cinnamon

1 egg

2 tablespoons natural peanut butter

Zest of 1 lime and juice of ½

¼ cup (15 g) roughly chopped cilantro

½ cup (30 g) panko or coarse bread crumbs

1. Heat 1 tablespoon of the oil in a large, lidded sauté pan over medium heat. Add the scallions and cook until they just begin to soften, about 2 minutes. Add the garlic, ginger, and chile and stir for 30 seconds, until fragrant. Stir in the carrots, salt, coriander, turmeric, and cinnamon. Cover and cook for 6 to 8 minutes, until the carrots are soft but not mushy.

2. In a mixing bowl, whisk together the egg, peanut butter, and lime zest and juice. Stir in the carrot mixture and the cilantro. Fold in the panko. Let stand for about 10 minutes, so the panko soaks up some of the moisture. Adjust seasonings. Shape into 4 patties, about ⅓ cup (60 g) each.

3. To cook (see pages 23–24 for detailed cooking instructions), warm a wide skillet over medium heat, then add the remaining oil. Add as many burgers as will fit comfortably without crowding the pan (usually 3 burgers will fit into a 10-inch/25 cm skillet), and cook until browned and crisped on the bottom, 5 to 7 minutes, then flip and repeat on the other side. The burgers will firm up a bit as they cook, and further once they're removed from the heat and have cooled slightly. Serve warm.

Mushroom Burgers with Barley Ⓥ

Makes four 4-inch (10 cm) burgers

These are some of my favorite veggie burgers in this book, in large part because they have such a pure flavor—it really tastes like a mushroom barley soup! Originally, I called for only barley, but I have found in subsequent years that farro works equally well; and if you have leftover cooked grains on hand, any chewy, substantial ones will do. You'll need about 1¼ cups (195 g). And any assortment of mushrooms works great. Because shiitakes have such a distinctive texture, chewier than buttons or cremini, I recommend using a few of them, but since they'll all be chopped up finely (either by hand or in your food processor), you won't want to bring out any of your show-stopping, hand-foraged gems for a recipe like this.

½ cup (100 g) pearled barley or farro (or leftover cooked grains; see headnote)

1 small potato, peeled and cut into ½-inch (1.25 cm) pieces

3 tablespoons olive oil

1½ pounds (680 g) assorted mushrooms (button, cremini, shiitake, portobellos)

½ teaspoon dried thyme

2 tablespoons balsamic vinegar

2 teaspoons potato starch, cornstarch, or arrowroot powder

½ teaspoon salt

¼ teaspoon freshly ground black pepper

1. Combine the barley with at least 3 cups (720 ml) water in a saucepan and bring to a boil. Reduce the heat to establish a simmer, then cook until the barley is tender—use your package instructions as a guide, but start tasting for doneness after about 18 minutes.

2. Bring about 1 inch (2.5 cm) of water to simmer in a small saucepan, then add the potato, cover the pan, and cook until the potato is tender. Drain off the liquid, then mash with a fork.

3. Coarsely chop the mushrooms, then transfer to the bowl of a food processor (in batches, if necessary) and pulse until they're finely minced. (You can also mince the mushrooms by hand.)

4. Warm 1 tablespoon of the oil in a wide skillet over medium heat. Add the mushrooms and thyme, and cook until the mushrooms release their liquid and it cooks off, 10 to 15 minutes. Pour in the vinegar and use a wooden spoon or spatula to scrape up any browned bits.

5. Combine the mushroom mixture with the potato, the barley, and the potato starch, salt, and pepper in a mixing bowl. Shape into 6 patties.

6. To cook (see pages 23–24 for detailed cooking instructions), warm a wide skillet over medium heat, then add the remaining oil. Add as many burgers as will fit comfortably without crowding the pan (usually 3 burgers will fit into a 10-inch/25 cm skillet), and cook until browned and crisped on the bottom, 3 to 5 minutes, then flip and repeat on the other side. Serve warm.

Beet "Tartare" ⓖⒻ

Makes five or six 3.5-inch (9 cm) "burgers"

This is a bit of a wild card, but I insist on including it, because who else but a French chef would take the creative challenge of a veggie burger and think "tartare"? The inspiration for this surprising burger—named more for its presentation than the method, since we are cooking the beets—comes from chef Pascal Bonhomme of Pascalou, a bistro on Manhattan's Upper East Side, where I used to wait tables. He is a whiz with the microwave, evidenced by the instructions below. You'll need five or six 4-ounce ramekins, though you can also cook in batches with fewer ramekins or use a metal ½-cup (118 ml) measuring cup as a ramekin. This is good with any variety of beets—red, gold, or Chioggia—but you'll only get the true "tartare" effect with the dark purple ones.

5 medium beets, scrubbed clean and trimmed of stems and fibrous roots

2 teaspoons olive oil, plus more for greasing

1 egg white

1 small shallot, minced, plus more for serving

2 teaspoons sherry vinegar

2 teaspoons minced fresh tarragon, plus additional leaves for serving

1 teaspoon potato starch or cornstarch

Crumbled goat cheese

Freshly ground black pepper

1. To roast the beets, preheat the oven to 400°F (200°C). Place the beets on a square of aluminum foil and rub with the oil. Wrap tightly in the foil. Roast for 45 minutes to 1 hour, until completely tender. Allow to cool completely. Peel the beets and chop into small dice—approximately ⅛ inch (3 mm).

2. In a mixing bowl, whisk together the egg white, shallot, vinegar, tarragon, and potato starch. Fold in the beets.

3. Line the bottom of each ramekin with a small circle of parchment paper. Oil the sides of each ramekin and the parchment. Pack each ramekin with the beet mixture, leveling off the top for a flat surface. Depending on the size of your beets, you will have enough to fill 5 or 6 ramekins.

4. Cover each ramekin with microwave-safe plastic wrap and microwave for 1 minute, until firmed. Alternatively, steam the ramekins: Bring ½ inch (1.25 cm) water to a simmer in a stockpot or saucepan with a colander or steaming basket insert. Add the ramekins (in batches, if necessary), cover, and steam the beet "burgers" for 3 minutes, until the mixture firms.

5. Let the ramekins cool to room temperature. (At this stage they can be refrigerated for up to 2 days.) Run a thin, sharp knife around the perimeter of each ramekin to loosen the beet mixture, and invert onto a serving plate. It will come out in a single, patty-shaped piece. Remove the parchment.

6. To serve, top each "burger" with goat cheese and black pepper to taste. Garnish with a few sprigs of tarragon and some minced shallot.

DO AHEAD: Roast beets

Tortilla-Crusted Stuffed Portobello Burgers

Makes four 4-inch (10 cm) burgers

This burger is inspired by the indulgent, unique veggie burger at Alias, a now-closed restaurant that was on Manhattan's Lower East Side. It's formed by two portobello mushrooms that sandwich a thick slice of queso blanco and a layer of puréed black beans, then crusted with panko and deep-fried. I use tortilla chip crumbs instead of panko and have lightened it up a bit with a baking method, but this is still a burger worth writing home about. It's great on a big, soft bun and topped with pico de gallo and fresh avocado slices. Use the smallest portobello mushrooms you can find; if they are too large, the burger becomes unwieldy.

8 small portobello mushrooms

3 cups (78 g) plain tortilla chips

1 cup (255 g) cooked black beans

4 ounces queso blanco, cheddar, or vegan alternative cheese (about ½ cup/113 g, crumbled or grated)

1 teaspoon salt

3 tablespoons white rice flour or all-purpose flour

¼ cup (60 ml) olive oil

1. Preheat the oven to 400°F (200°C). Lightly grease a baking sheet.

2. Trim the stems from the mushrooms and scrape out the gills with a spoon. Place the caps, rounded sides up, on the prepared baking sheet. Roast, flipping every 5 minutes, for 15 to 20 minutes, until the mushrooms are tender and have released most of their liquid. Allow to cool.

3. Reduce the oven temperature to 350°F (177°C).

4. In the bowl of a food processor, pulse the tortilla chips until uniformly ground. Transfer the crumbs to a shallow bowl and set aside. Add the black beans, queso blanco, and ½ teaspoon of the salt to the food processor and purée.

5. To assemble the burgers, sandwich 2 heaping tablespoons of the bean mixture between 2 roasted mushrooms. Repeat, to make 4 burgers.

6. Combine the flour, the remaining salt, and 6 tablespoons water in a second shallow bowl, and whisk to combine—it should be thin enough to easily coat the burgers. Dredge each burger in the flour slurry, allowing the excess to drip off, then coat with tortilla crumbs.

7. Heat the oil in an oven-safe skillet or nonstick sauté pan over medium heat. Add the burgers and cook for 6 to 10 minutes, until golden on each side. Transfer the pan to the oven and bake for 10 to 12 minutes, until the burger exteriors are uniformly browned and the breading fully firmed. Serve warm.

Carrot-Parsnip Burgers with Almonds Ⓥ Ⓖ🄵

Makes six 4-inch (10 cm) burgers

Along with my Beet and Hazelnut Burgers (page 78), these were my inaugural burger mixes. I developed this recipe while working at 61 Local, in Cobble Hill, Brooklyn, where the proprietor, Dave Liatti, generously allowed me to use his kitchen and add my burgers to the menu so as to gauge customer thoughts. Over time, I removed the almonds from the recipe, in order to make them a bit more versatile, flavor-wise. But the way the floral notes of the almonds and parsnips complement each other is something I still enjoy, and so it's always a pleasure to return to this original pairing.

¼ cup (45 g) quinoa, rinsed if not prerinsed

1 teaspoon salt

4 tablespoons olive oil

1 small onion, diced

2 cloves garlic

1 large or 2 medium carrots, coarsely grated

1 medium or 2 small parsnips, coarsely grated

1 tablespoon apple cider vinegar

¼ cup (15 g) potato flakes

1 teaspoon cornstarch, potato starch, or arrowroot powder

½ cup (55 g) toasted almonds, finely chopped or ground

1. Combine the quinoa with ½ cup (120 ml) water in a small saucepan and bring to a boil. Add ¼ teaspoon of the salt, then reduce the heat to low and cover the pan. Cook gently for 18 to 20 minutes, until the water is absorbed, the grains are tender, and the germ of the quinoa is exposed. Set aside, uncovered, to cool as you prepare the remaining ingredients.

2. Heat 2 tablespoons of the oil in a medium skillet over medium heat. Add the onion and remaining salt, and cook until the onions are softened and beginning to caramelize, about 7 to 10 minutes. Add the garlic, stirring until fragrant, then add the carrots and parsnips. Cook, stirring periodically, until the vegetables are tender and have concentrated and collapsed a bit, 6 to 10 minutes. Some caramelization and blistering is good! Deglaze the pan with the vinegar, using a wooden spoon to scrape any browned bits, then scrape the mixture into a mixing bowl and set aside to cool slightly.

3. Stir the quinoa into the vegetable mixture, along with the potato flakes, cornstarch, and almonds. Shape into 6 medium burgers.

4. To cook (see pages 23–24 for detailed cooking instructions), warm a wide skillet over medium heat, then add the remaining oil. Add as many burgers as will fit comfortably without crowding the pan (usually 3 burgers will fit into a 10-inch/25 cm skillet), and cook until browned and crisped on the bottom, 5 to 7 minutes, then flip and repeat on the other side. The burgers will firm up a bit as they cook, and further once they're removed from the heat and have cooled slightly. Serve warm.

Baked Cauliflower Burgers

Makes six 4-inch (10 cm) burgers

Farmers market cauliflower has a natural sweetness that's much more readily apparent than in the plastic-wrapped ones found year-round at the supermarket, and I really notice the difference in burgers like this one. Modeling it a bit after a cauliflower dish I remember eating a lot growing up—where it was boiled whole, then draped with a mustardy cheese sauce and broiled—I've paired it with tangy Dijon mustard and capers. Serve with a slice of Swiss or Gruyère cheese for something richer.

1 medium head cauliflower, cut into large florets

3 tablespoons Dijon mustard

2 tablespoons potato starch

2 eggs

Squeeze of fresh lemon juice

¼ cup (15 g) roughly chopped parsley

2 tablespoons capers, drained, rinsed, and roughly chopped

¼ teaspoon red pepper flakes

1¼ teaspoons salt

1½ cups (90 g) panko or coarse bread crumbs

¼ cup (20 g) finely grated Parmesan

1. Preheat the oven to 350°F (177°C). Line a baking sheet with parchment paper.

2. Bring 1 inch (2.5 cm) water to a simmer in a small saucepan. Place the cauliflower in a steaming basket and set inside the saucepan, cover, and steam for 8 to 10 minutes, until the cauliflower can be easily pierced with a knife. Cool slightly on a baking sheet or cutting board.

3. In a food processor, purée two thirds of the steamed cauliflower with the mustard, potato starch, eggs, and lemon juice, until well combined and mostly smooth. Transfer to a large mixing bowl.

4. Chop the remaining cauliflower into ⅛- to ¼-inch (3–6 mm) pieces (or pulse in a food processor until roughly chopped). Add to the puréed mixture. Stir in the parsley, capers, red pepper flakes, and ½ teaspoon of the salt. Fold in 1 cup (60 g) of the panko. Adjust seasonings. Shape into 6 patties.

5. Combine the remaining panko, the remaining salt, and the Parmesan on a plate. Gently dredge the patties in the crumbs so they are coated on both sides and on the edges. Place on the prepared baking sheet. Bake for 20 to 25 minutes, flipping halfway through, until the burgers are firm and uniformly browned. Serve warm.

Butternut Squash and Black Bean Burgers Ⓥ

Makes six 4-inch (10 cm) burgers

Squash and beans are a combination I always love in soups, salads, tacos, and burritos, and it's no surprise that the two ingredients also work great together in a veggie burger. These burgers are excellent with a slice of mozzarella or melty vegan cheese, which adds richness and some extra structural support on a bun. And since the beans and bit of starch do all the work in terms of binding the burger, I recommend the "Smash Burger" cooking method, detailed on pages 23–24. Also, since the recipe only calls for half a butternut squash, you might as well roast the other half at the same time and use it for soup.

1 onion

½ medium butternut squash, split lengthwise from the stem

2 tablespoons plus 1 teaspoon olive oil

5 ounces (150 g) spinach, fresh or frozen

1½ cups (255 g) cooked black beans

2 teaspoons potato starch, cornstarch, or arrowroot powder

1 teaspoon salt

⅓ cup (20 g) panko or coarse bread crumbs, plus additional if needed

1. Preheat the oven to 400°F (200°C). Line a baking sheet with aluminum foil.

2. Peel and quarter the onion along the stem, leaving the base attached to each quarter so that it holds its shape. Rub the onion and the squash with the 1 teaspoon oil, and arrange on the baking sheet, with the squash lying flat. Roast for 25 to 35 minutes, flipping the squash twice so that it finishes facedown, until both the onion and the squash are completely tender. If the onion begins to burn while the squash is still cooking, remove it from the pan. Allow to cool until safe to handle.

3. Meanwhile, prepare the spinach. If using fresh spinach, steam it for 3 to 4 minutes over 1 inch (2.5 cm) of simmering water or blanch it for 30 seconds in a pot of boiling salted water. Transfer to an ice bath to halt the cooking. Squeeze dry and finely chop. If using frozen spinach, allow it to thaw (you can speed this up in the microwave, or by dropping it in a saucepan of simmering water), and once cool, squeeze dry and finely chop.

4. Scoop out the seeds and peel the skin off the squash, then measure out 1 packed cup (205 g) of flesh. Reserve the rest for another use. Trim the base from the onions. In the bowl of a food processor, combine the onions, the squash, and the spinach. Pulse until just combined. Add the beans, potato starch, and salt, and pulse several times until combined. Add the panko, and pulse until integrated. (Alternatively, chop the

onions by hand and mash the squash with a fork or potato masher.) Add additional panko if the mixture seems too wet to become malleable. Shape into 6 patties, then let stand for at least 20 minutes.

5. To cook (see pages 23–24 for detailed cooking instructions), warm a wide skillet over medium-high heat, then add the remaining oil. Add as many burgers as will fit comfortably without crowding the pan (usually 3 burgers will fit into a 10-inch/25 cm skillet), and use a metal spatula to flatten them slightly. Cook until browned and crisped on the bottom, 5 to 7 minutes, then flip and repeat on the other side. The burgers will firm up a bit as they cook, and further once they're removed from the heat and have cooled slightly. Serve warm.

Beet and Hazelnut Burgers Ⓥ ⒼⒻ

Makes six 4-inch (10 cm) burgers

This was the first veggie burger flavor I launched with my company Made by Lukas. I'm very proud of this recipe, which is vegan, gluten-free, full of flavor, and boasts a terrific texture, too. I love the floral flavor of the hazelnuts here, and it's important to freshly toast them to get the most bang for your buck; in fact, I recommend toasting them *well*, to a dark, chestnut shade of brown, which will also contribute some pleasantly crunchy texture. And while these burgers taste nothing like meat—they taste like beets! which is the whole idea—the mixture might seem alarmingly red to the unsuspecting guest in your kitchen.

¼ cup (45 g) quinoa, rinsed if
    not prerinsed

1 teaspoon salt

2 small- to medium-size beets

1 large or 2 medium carrots

4 tablespoons olive oil

1 small onion, diced

1 teaspoon ground cumin

2 cloves garlic

1 tablespoon red
    wine vinegar

¼ cup (15 g) potato flakes

1 teaspoon cornstarch, potato
    starch, or arrowroot powder

½ cup (55 g) toasted hazelnuts,
    finely chopped or ground

1. Combine the quinoa with ½ cup (120 ml) water in a small saucepan and bring to a boil. Add ¼ teaspoon of the salt, then reduce the heat to low and cover the pan. Cook gently for 18 to 20 minutes, until the water is absorbed, the grains are tender, and the germ of the quinoa is exposed. Set aside, uncovered, to cool as you prepare the remaining ingredients.

2. Scrub the beets and carrots. Trim off the ends and any stringy bits from the beets, but it's not necessary to peel them. Grate both vegetables using the large holes on a box grater.

3. Heat 2 tablespoons of the oil in a medium skillet over medium heat. Add the onion, cumin, and the remaining salt, and cook until the onions are softened and beginning to caramelize, about 7 to 10 minutes. Add the garlic, stirring until fragrant, then add the beets and carrots. Cook, stirring periodically, until the vegetables are tender and have concentrated and collapsed a bit, 6 to 10 minutes. Some caramelization and blistering on the carrots and beets is good! Deglaze the pan with the vinegar, using a wooden spoon to scrape any browned bits, then scrape the mixture into a mixing bowl and set aside to cool slightly.

4. Stir the quinoa into the vegetable mixture, along with the potato flakes, cornstarch, and hazelnuts. Shape into 6 medium burgers.

5. To cook (see pages 23–24 for detailed cooking instructions), place a wide skillet over medium heat, and once warm, add the remaining oil. Add as many burgers as will fit comfortably without crowding the pan (usually 3 burgers will fit into a 10-inch/25 cm skillet), and cook until browned and crisped on the bottom, 5 to 7 minutes, then flip and repeat on the other side. The burgers will firm up a bit as they cook, and further once they're removed from the heat and have cooled slightly. Serve warm.

Spinach-Chickpea Burgers ⓖⒻ

Makes five 4-inch (10 cm) burgers

This veggie burger features so many of my favorite things in a veggie burger: hearty chickpeas, fortifying spinach, a hint of nutty toasted cumin seeds, and final finish of fresh lemon. It's also very easy. As with most burgers in this book, be sure to add the beans in two stages, to create texture in the finished burger. I like to serve them accompanied by traditional burger fixings: lettuce, tomato, and mustard.

2 tablespoons plus 1 teaspoon olive oil

1 teaspoon cumin seeds, toasted and ground

5 ounces (150 g) fresh spinach

1½ cups (255 g) cooked chickpeas

2 eggs

Juice of ½ lemon

1 teaspoon salt

⅓ cup (30 g) chickpea flour, or more if needed

1. Heat the 1 teaspoon oil in a medium skillet over medium heat. Add the cumin and spinach and cook, tossing with tongs, until the spinach is completely wilted, 2 or 3 minutes. Transfer to a heat-safe plate and allow to cool until safe to handle. Drain if necessary, wrap in a towel, and squeeze out as much liquid as possible. Chop finely.

2. In the bowl of a food processor, combine 1¼ cups (213 g) of the chickpeas, the eggs, lemon juice, and salt. Pulse until the mixture resembles a chunky hummus. Add the spinach, the remaining chickpeas, and the chickpea flour, pulsing to combine but leaving some texture intact. The mixture should be sticky but somewhat pliable. If too wet, add more flour, 1 teaspoon at a time; if too dry, add a bit of water. Shape into 5 patties, and let stand for at least 20 minutes (and up to a few hours in the refrigerator).

3. To cook (see pages 23–24 for detailed cooking instructions), warm a wide skillet over medium heat, then add the remaining oil. Add as many burgers as will fit comfortably without crowding the pan (usually 3 burgers will fit into a 10-inch/25 cm skillet), and cook until browned and crisped on the bottom, 5 to 7 minutes, then flip and repeat on the other side. The burgers will firm up a bit as they cook, and further once they're removed from the heat and have cooled slightly. Serve warm.

Sweet Potato Burgers with Lentils and Kale

Makes six 4-inch (10 cm) burgers

This is a hearty, nutritious burger, inspired by one of my favorite trios of vegetables to use for a fall-to-winter soup. Use any hearty green you like or have on hand, including chard, beet greens, turnip greens, or mature spinach. Likewise, if you have a leftover roasted sweet potato, use it instead of the steamed potato. The burgers are delicious topped with any of the yogurt sauces (pages 162–63). To veganize these burgers, my favorite substitute is a steamed starchy potato plus potato starch (see pages 18 for more information)—and you can steam it along with the sweet potato.

¾ cup (150 g) French (green) lentils

1 bunch kale, tough stems removed

1 medium sweet potato, peeled and chopped into 1-inch (2.5 cm) pieces

4 tablespoons olive oil

1 medium onion, diced

1½ teaspoons garam masala

1½ teaspoons curry powder

Pinch of cayenne pepper

3 garlic cloves

1 egg, beaten

3 tablespoons chopped fresh cilantro

½ teaspoon salt

Squeeze of fresh lime juice

⅓ cup (20 g) panko or coarse bread crumbs, plus additional if needed

1. To cook the lentils, pick through the lentils and rinse thoroughly. Combine the lentils and at least 3 cups (720 ml) water in a small saucepan and bring to a boil. Cover, reduce the heat, and simmer for 15 to 20 minutes, until tender. Drain and then transfer lentils to a large mixing bowl. Coarsely mash them with a potato masher.

2. Meanwhile, steam the kale. Bring 1 inch (2.5 cm) water to a simmer in a saucepan. Place the kale in a steaming basket and set inside the saucepan, cover, and steam for 5 to 8 minutes, until completely tender. Transfer to a plate or cutting board. Allow to cool until safe to handle. Grab in fistfuls and squeeze out as much liquid as possible. Finely chop and set aside.

3. Place the sweet potato in the steaming basket, adding more water if necessary. Cover and cook for 8 to 10 minutes, until the potato is completely tender. Add the potato to the lentils, mashing thoroughly with a fork or potato masher.

4. Heat 2 tablespoons of the oil in a sauté pan over medium heat. Add the onion, garam masala, curry powder, and cayenne, and cook until the onion is soft, golden, and sweet, 10 to 12 minutes. Add the kale and the garlic. Cook for about 2 minutes, tossing to combine. If a crust has formed on the base of the pan, add 2 tablespoons water and scrape up the browned bits with a wooden spoon.

5. Combine the kale-onion mixture with the lentil mixture. Stir in the egg, cilantro, salt, and lime juice. Fold in the panko, adding additional panko if needed. Adjust seasonings. Shape into 6 patties.

6. To cook (see pages 23–24 for detailed cooking instructions), warm a wide skillet over medium heat, then add the remaining oil. Add as many burgers as will fit comfortably without crowding the pan (usually 3 burgers will fit into a 10-inch/25 cm skillet), and cook until browned and crisped on the bottom, 5 to 7 minutes, then flip and repeat on the other side. The burgers will firm up a bit as they cook, and further once they're removed from the heat and have cooled slightly. Serve warm.

Corn Burgers with Sun-Dried Tomatoes and Goat Cheese

Makes six 5-inch (13 cm) burgers

This utterly delicious burger is part flapjack, part veggie burger. It's too wet to shape into patties—you just drop a big spoonful of the mixture into a hot sauté pan. Try it as a savory breakfast, topped with a fried egg, as the base for a simple salad, or on a crusty wheat roll topped with goat cheese and hot sauce.

1½ cups (248 g) fresh or frozen corn kernels

2 eggs

½ cup (78 g) stone-ground cornmeal or polenta

¼ cup (30 g) all-purpose flour

2 teaspoons cornstarch

½ teaspoon baking powder

6 scallions, including 1 inch (2.5 cm) into the dark green parts, thinly sliced

½ cup (55 g) oil-packed sun-dried tomatoes, diced

½ teaspoon salt

¼ teaspoon freshly ground black pepper

3 ounces (85 g) goat cheese

2 tablespoons olive oil

1. In the bowl of a food processor or in a blender, combine 1 cup (165 g) of the corn and the eggs. Pulse until it's the texture of chunky hummus, not completely liquefied.

2. In a mixing bowl, whisk together the cornmeal, flour, cornstarch, and baking powder. Stir in the remaining corn, the corn-egg mixture, the scallions, sun-dried tomatoes, salt, and pepper. Crumble the goat cheese over the corn mixture and fold it in.

3. Heat the oil in a sauté pan over medium heat. Drop the mixture by heaping ¼-cup (124 g) portions into the hot skillet, pressing gently with a spatula to round them into burger shapes. Cook until golden brown on the bottoms, 4 to 5 minutes (lower the heat if they cook too quickly). Carefully flip and cook until browned and firmed in the centers, another 4 or 5 minutes. Serve hot or warm.

Curried Eggplant and Tomato Burgers Ⓥ ⓖⒻ

Makes four 4-inch (10 cm) burgers

Curry spices give these burgers a sweet, complex heat. If you can't find a Japanese eggplant, use a baby eggplant or the smaller Italian eggplant–too much eggplant will add too much water to this recipe. I love these burgers as sliders. They're wonderful freshly cooked, but they firm up very nicely when cooled, such that they make an excellent on-the-road snack, packed up in a container for lunch, or an appetizer for your favorite yogurt sauce. Slather with Spiced Tomato Relish (page 158) and top with a handful of Frizzled Shallots (page 152).

1 small Japanese or Italian eggplant

1 cup (150 g) cherry tomatoes

1 medium Yukon Gold potato, peeled and chopped

1½ cups (300 g) cooked brown rice

1 small red onion, finely chopped

3 garlic cloves, minced

2 tablespoons roughly chopped cilantro

1 teaspoon curry powder

1 teaspoon garam masala

½ teaspoon molasses

½ teaspoon salt

Pinch of cayenne pepper

2 teaspoons potato starch

1. Preheat the oven's broiler on its high heat setting. Line a baking sheet with aluminum foil.

2. Prick the eggplant all over with a fork. Place the eggplant and tomatoes on opposite ends of the prepared baking sheet. Broil, stirring the tomatoes and flipping the eggplant every 4 minutes, until the eggplant is collapsed and tender all over, and the tomatoes have burst and begun to shrivel, usually 8 to 12 minutes. If one vegetable cooks before the other, remove it and set aside, then return the pan to the broiler. Allow the eggplant to cool until it is safe to handle, then remove the skin by peeling it off in long strips. Coarsely chop the tomatoes and eggplant. (The roasted vegetables can be covered and refrigerated for up to 2 days at this point.)

3. Bring 1 inch (2.5 cm) of water to a simmer in a small saucepan. Place the potato in a steaming basket and set inside the saucepan, cover, and cook until it's completely tender, 8 to 10 minutes. Remove and allow to cool.

4. Reduce the oven temperature to 375°F (190°C). Line a baking sheet with parchment paper.

5. In a mixing bowl, use a fork to mash the potato, then add the eggplant and tomatoes, then the rice, onion, garlic, cilantro, curry powder, garam masala, molasses, salt, cayenne, and potato starch. This is a somewhat loose mixture, so you won't be able to easily shape it into patties. Rather, divide it into 4 portions on the prepared baking sheet and shape into patties.

6. Transfer the pan to the oven and bake for 15 minutes, until the burgers are firmed and cooked through. Serve warm.

DO AHEAD: Roast tomatoes and eggplant

Tofu, Seitan, Tempeh, and TVP Burgers

Tofu, seitan, tempeh, and textured vegetable protein (TVP) bring a boost of protein to any veggie burger. Even more so than beans, they are a blank canvas for you to take in any direction because they really acquire the flavors of the ingredients they are paired with. They lend themselves particularly to Asian-inspired burgers, but when used correctly they can enhance almost any patty. Follow a few guidelines and you'll find them to be delicious base for all types of veggie burgers.

TOFU

In a process that's similar to cheese, tofu is made from coagulated soy milk, and I find it to be the most obvious choice of a protein base for veggie burgers in this chapter. Because of its soft, spongy texture, it doubles as a primary protein and can also function as a binder. I used to make burgers by blending tofu in a food processor but never really loved it because that compromised all its structural integrity. So my favorite way to manipulate it into a burger is to blend a portion of the tofu, which has helpful binding properties, and coarsely grate the rest.

To prepare tofu for cooking, you'll need to drain and dry it. If using firm or extra-firm tofu (which is recommended in these recipes), the tofu can be cut into thick slices, placed between a few layers of paper towels, and weighed down with something heavy, like a cutting board or a skillet and a few cans of beans.

To store leftover tofu, cover with fresh water and keep in the refrigerator. If you change the water daily, it should last up to three or four days. You'll notice an off smell, somewhat sour like spoiled milk, when it has gone bad.

SEITAN

Seitan is the product of cooking wheat gluten, which is the resulting protein after thoroughly rinsing and stripping wheat of all its starch. There are plenty of good premade seitan brands on the market, both vacuum- and water-packed (and sometimes in cans). But I think you'll discover that it's very fun to make on your own (see the seitan burger on page 98). Seitan has the dense, chewy texture of meat—this is what you're getting when you order "vegetarian duck" at a Chinese or Thai restaurant—and if prepared correctly, it can taste disarmingly similar.

When you sauté it, seitan browns and crispens, and whatever sauces you are cooking it in will caramelize on the exterior. In the seitan burger, it is literally used as a slab of protein slathered in barbecue sauce.

TEMPEH

An Indonesian, plant-based protein that's made from cultured, fermented soybeans, tempeh is often used to make vegan approximations of meat staples, such as veggie burgers, bacon, and sausage. It has a more robust nutritional profile and higher protein content than tofu or seitan—its protein levels are similar to those found in many meats, and it's incredibly nutritious even beyond its protein content. For those who didn't grow up with tempeh and aren't familiar, its firm texture can be very appealing, but you may need some time to acquire an appreciation for its flavor. Western treatments of tempeh often involve heavy-handed seasonings to mask its flavor. But given its easy preparation and incredible nutritional offering, it's a good one to develop an appreciation for.

Cooking tempeh removes the slightly sour taste it has when raw. In the recipes here, it is sautéed before being made into a burger, but it can also be steamed. Many prepared tempeh brands contain additional grains and seeds like wild rice and flax. Be sure to select a variety that will complement the other ingredients in your burger.

Chipotle Black Bean Burgers ⓥ

Makes six 4-inch (10 cm) burgers

Textured vegetable protein (TVP), which is simply dried soy flakes, has fallen out of favor in vegetarian home cooking, though it's quite common in processed vegan burgers and other prepared foods. Health food stores often carry it in the bulk bins. In select instances, such as this recipe, it can be an efficient way to make a heartier burger. It needs to be reconstituted before it can be cooked. The ratio is almost 1:1 water to TVP; I have better results when about 1 tablespoon less water is used for every 1 cup (227 g) of TVP. This vegan burger takes its inspiration from the frozen black bean burgers I used to eat. It's great on a bun and added to a cookout spread (see page 24 for my tips on grilling veggie burgers), but to my mind, it has breakfast vibes, and I like it at that time of day with some avocado slices and a couple shakes of hot sauce.

¾ cup (170 g) textured vegetable protein (TVP)

⅔ cup (160 ml) boiling water

3 tablespoons oil

½ onion, roughly chopped

½ cup (83 g) fresh or frozen corn kernels

1 or 2 chipotle chile peppers in adobo sauce, minced, plus 1 tablespoon sauce

1½ cups (255 g) cooked black beans

1 cup (200 g) cooked brown rice

¼ cup (15 g) chopped cilantro

2 teaspoons potato starch, cornstarch, or arrowroot powder

Juice of 1 lime

1 teaspoon salt

⅓ cup (20 g) panko or coarse bread crumbs, plus more if needed

1. Place the TVP in a small bowl, pour over the boiling water, and let stand for 10 minutes.

2. Warm a skillet over medium heat, then add 1 tablespoon of the oil, followed by the onion. Cook until soft and translucent, 6 to 8 minutes, then stir in the corn, chiles, and adobe sauce. Cook for 1 to 2 minutes more, then remove from the heat.

3. Use a potato masher or fork to mash the beans. Add the onion and corn mixture, the reconstituted TVP mixture, and the rice, cilantro, starch, lime juice, salt, and panko, stirring to combine, using your hands if needed to mash the mixture together. Let stand for at least 20 minutes, and up to a few hours in the refrigerator, then shape into 6 patties.

4. To cook (see pages 23–24 for detailed cooking instructions), warm a wide skillet over medium heat, then add the remaining oil. Add as many burgers as will fit comfortably without crowding the pan (usually 3 burgers will fit into a 10-inch/25 cm skillet), and gently flatten using a metal spatula. Cook until browned and crisped on the bottom, 5 to 7 minutes, then flip and repeat on the other side. The burgers will firm up a bit as they cook, and further once they're removed from the heat and have cooled slightly. Serve warm.

WaterCourse Foods Tempeh Burgers 🅥 🅖🅕

Makes six 4-inch (10 cm) burgers

WaterCourse Foods in Denver, Colorado, a long-standing vegan comfort food restaurant, has a locally revered veggie burger. Their recipe has since changed, but chef Rachel Kresley and manager Callie Liddell graciously offered this earlier iteration for this book's first edition—it uses tempeh to delicious effect. It's a study in umami, with Worcestershire, arame, and liquid smoke uniting to create something that one can only call—and I don't use this word very often when it comes to veggie burgers—meaty. It's a bit of a project, but worth it.

½ cup (90 g) wild rice

1 tablespoon olive oil

½ onion, diced

1 stalk celery, diced

1 carrot, diced

½ red bell pepper, diced

2 garlic cloves, minced

1 teaspoon dried parsley

½ teaspoon ground cumin

¼ teaspoon onion powder

¼ teaspoon garlic powder

¼ teaspoon ground fennel

1 teaspoon salt

¼ teaspoon freshly ground black pepper

One 8-ounce (277 g) package tempeh

2 teaspoons fresh lemon juice

2 teaspoons soy sauce or tamari (GF)

2 teaspoons apple cider vinegar

1 teaspoon liquid smoke

½ teaspoon vegan Worcestershire sauce (GF)

2 tablespoon arame, rehydrated according to package directions, drained, and chopped

1 tablespoon nutritional yeast

½ cup (45 g) chickpea flour

1. Combine the rice and 1¼ cups (300 ml) water in a small saucepan and bring to a boil. Reduce the heat, cover, and cook for 40 to 50 minutes, until the water is completely absorbed. Continue cooking for 10 minutes longer, so as to overcook the rice; you want a mushy texture. Transfer to a baking sheet and cool completely.

2. Preheat the oven to 400°F (200°C). Line a baking sheet with parchment paper.

3. Heat the oil in a medium sauté pan over medium heat. Add the onion, celery, carrot, and bell pepper and cook until softened, 6 to 8 minutes. Add the garlic, parsley, cumin, onion powder, garlic powder, fennel, salt, and pepper. Crumble the tempeh over the vegetable mixture. Sauté for 5 minutes over low heat. Add the lemon juice, soy sauce, vinegar, liquid smoke, and Worcestershire, and deglaze, scraping up the browned bits with a wooden spoon. Cook until the liquid is fully absorbed, 3 to 5 minutes. Transfer to a mixing bowl and allow to cool until safe to handle. Add the rice and the arame and nutritional yeast, mixing with your hands.

4. In the bowl of a food processor, pulse half the mixture until uniformly puréed. Return it to the bowl with the remaining mixture and stir in the chickpea flour. The mixture will be dense and sticky. Shape into 6 patties and place on the prepared baking sheet.

5. Bake for 20 minutes, flipping the patties and rotating the pan halfway through, until firm and cooked through. Serve warm.

Tofu and Chard Burgers ⓥ

Makes six 4-inch (10 cm) burgers

Here's a well-seasoned tofu burger, updated to reflect my preferred tofu burger technique, which combines blended and coarsely grated tofu. Feel free to substitute kale, beet greens, spinach, or any other dark leafy greens for the chard here, but chard is my preference because I just love their stems and think that they're underappreciated by most home cooks. Don't toss the stems! You'll use half of them in this recipe—think of them as a stand-in for celery—and reserve the rest for stir-fries and sautés, or roast them until crispy, in which case they make a great snack.

One 14- to 16-ounce (397–454 g) block firm tofu

1 bunch chard, leaves and stems separated

4 tablespoons olive oil

1 teaspoon grated fresh ginger

2 garlic cloves, minced

3 tablespoons soy sauce or tamari (GF)

1 teaspoon agave nectar

2 teaspoons sesame oil

¾ cup (45 g) panko or coarse bread crumbs

Sweet Sesame Glaze, optional (page 159)

1. Drain the tofu. Cut in half lengthwise, then wrap both pieces in a clean kitchen towel or a few layers of paper towel and set a broad, flat weight on top (a cutting board works great). Let stand for about 10 minutes. Coarsely grate one piece of the tofu.

2. Thinly slice half the chard stems as you would celery, reserving the rest for another use. Coarsely chop the leaves. Heat 1 tablespoon of the oil in a skillet over medium heat. Add the chard stems and cook until softened, 5 to 7 minutes, followed by the leaves. Cook, tossing with tongs, until fully wilted, about 2 minutes. Transfer to a plate. Allow to cool until safe to handle, then gently squeeze out as much liquid as possible. Finely chop.

3. Wipe out the skillet and place over medium-high heat. Add 1 tablespoon of the oil, followed by the grated tofu. Cook, stirring often, until it begins to lightly brown, then add the ginger and garlic, stirring until just fragrant, and then add the soy sauce, agave, and sesame oil. Cook until the liquid has reduced significantly and the pan seems mostly dry, 8 to 10 minutes. Stir in the chard, then remove from the heat and transfer to a mixing bowl.

4. In the bowl of a food processor, purée half the tofu, then transfer it to the mixing bowl and fold in the panko. Let stand for 5 to 10 minutes, so the panko soaks up as much moisture as possible. Shape into 6 patties.

5. To cook (see pages 23–24 for detailed cooking instructions), warm a wide skillet over medium heat, then add the remaining oil. Add as many burgers as will fit comfortably without crowding the pan (usually 3 burgers will fit into a 10-inch/25 cm skillet), and cook until browned and crisped on the bottom, 5 to 7 minutes, then flip and repeat on the other side. The burgers will firm up a bit as they cook, and further once they're removed from the heat and have cooled slightly. Serve warm.

6. If desired, drizzle with the sesame glaze just before serving.

Seitan Burgers with Mango BBQ Sauce Ⓥ

Makes six 4-inch (10 cm) burgers

I highly recommend making your own seitan for this recipe. It's a much easier process than you'd expect, and there's plenty of room for improvisation, in both making the cooking broth as well as the seitan itself. The Mango BBQ Sauce is also easy and delicious, but feel free to substitute your favorite barbecue sauce. Garnish with julienned cabbage, a handful of fresh cilantro or scallions, and sesame seeds on a Pretzel Roll (page 114)—the sauce's salty forthrightness holds its own against the savory seitan.

COOKING LIQUID

1 tablespoon toasted sesame oil

1 small onion, roughly chopped

6 mushrooms, halved, or a handful of mushroom stems and scraps

1-inch (2.5 cm) piece fresh ginger, thinly sliced

4 garlic cloves, crushed

¼ cup (60 g) soy sauce or tamari (GF)

SEITAN

1 cup (120 g) vital wheat gluten

1 teaspoon ground ginger

1 teaspoon garlic powder

2 tablespoons soy sauce

1 teaspoon toasted sesame oil

BURGERS

1 tablespoon olive oil

1 cup (240 g) Mango BBQ Sauce (page 159)

1. To prepare the cooking liquid, heat the sesame oil in a medium stockpot over medium heat. Add the onion, mushrooms, ginger, and garlic, tossing to combine. Cover and cook for about 2 minutes, until the onion just begins to sweat. Add 6 cups (1.5 L) water and the soy sauce. Bring to a boil, then reduce to a simmer. Partially cover, and simmer over low heat for up to 2 hours or until ready for the seitan.

2. To prepare the seitan, in a mixing bowl, whisk together the vital wheat gluten, ginger, and garlic powder. In a separate bowl, combine ⅔ cup (160 ml) water, the soy sauce, and the sesame oil. Add the wet ingredients to the dry, mixing with a wooden spoon until combined. It will be a fairly stiff, rubbery mixture. Don't worry if there's excess liquid in the bowl. Turn the mixture out on to a clean work surface and knead for 30 seconds. Let stand for 10 minutes, then knead for another 30 seconds. With a dough scraper or knife, divide into four sections. Gently stretch each piece with your hands until it resembles a cutlet.

3. Add the seitan pieces to the cooking broth. Cover the pot and simmer for 1 hour, turning the seitan every 15 minutes or so, until it is firm and has fully expanded. The seitan will expand a lot—add more hot water to the pot if needed. Remove the pot from the heat and store the seitan in its cooking liquid until ready to use.

4. To assemble the burgers, drain the seitan thoroughly and squeeze out some of the liquid. Cut into 1-inch (2.5 cm) pieces. Heat the oil in a large sauté pan or skillet

over medium-high heat. Add the seitan and sauté until browned, 8 to 10 minutes. Remove from the heat and add the BBQ sauce, tossing to combine. To serve, scoop the seitan mixture onto 6 rolls.

NOTE: Seitan can be made in advance and kept in water or cooking liquid for 1 week in the refrigerator, or for up to 3 months in the freezer. If refrigerating, change the water daily.

Smoked Tofu and Bean Burgers Ⓥ

Makes six 4-inch (10 cm) burgers

Smoked tofu makes this burger reminiscent of the best barbecued foods, and it can be an incredibly handy thing to keep around for quick meals, as it's already fully seasoned and drained—just slice it up and add to salads or stir-fries. Here it's sauteed and then pulsed in a food processor with beans and a few other aromatics, and the tofu lends texture and plenty of smoky flavor to the burgers. Top with grated raw carrot, a sprinkling of thinly sliced scallion, and a handful of fresh cilantro leaves.

3 tablespoons olive oil

1 medium onion, diced

1 garlic clove, minced

One 8-ounce (227 g) package smoked tofu, roughly diced

1½ cups (255 g) cooked black or red kidney beans

¼ cup (15 g) minced cilantro

2 teaspoons potato starch, cornstarch, or arrowroot powder

Juice of ½ lime

¼ teaspoon salt

Pinch of cayenne pepper

½ cup (30 g) panko or coarse bread crumbs

1. Heat a medium sauté pan over medium heat, then add 1 tablespoon of the oil. Add the onion and cook until translucent, 8 to 10 minutes. Stir in the garlic and cook until fragrant, 1 minute longer. Allow to cool slightly.

2. In the bowl of a food processor, combine the onion and the garlic with the tofu, beans, cilantro, potato starch, lime juice, salt, and cayenne. Process until combined and slightly chunky. Add the panko and pulse a few times, to just combine. Shape into 6 patties.

3. To cook (see pages 23–24 for detailed cooking instructions), warm a wide skillet over medium heat, then add the remaining oil. Add as many burgers as will fit comfortably without crowding the pan (usually 3 burgers will fit into a 10-inch/25 cm skillet), and cook until browned and crisped on the bottom, 5 to 7 minutes, then flip and repeat on the other side. The burgers will firm up a bit as they cook, and further once they're removed from the heat and have cooled slightly. Serve warm.

"Garden" Burgers

Makes six 4-inch (10 cm) burgers

Similar to the Chipotle Black Bean Burgers on page 92, this is my (improved) version of the Gardenburger found in the frozen aisle at the grocery store—which I have enjoyed many times, most often at diners in New York where I'd eat it with two slices of cheddar cheese and copious amounts of ketchup. There's plenty of room to improvise here. Throw in yellow squash instead of zucchini, and grated carrots or beets would be welcome, as would finely chopped broccoli, green beans, peas, or edamame. You'll just want to cook out the water in any vegetable you add, and keep the final volume of the cooked vegetables around 1¼ cups (175 g).

1 medium zucchini, grated

1¼ teaspoons salt

½ cup (113 g) textured vegetable protein (TVP)

⅓ cup (80 ml) hot water

3 tablespoons olive oil

1 medium onion, chopped

8 button or cremini mushrooms, thinly sliced

1 tablespoon tomato paste

2 tablespoons red or white wine vinegar

1½ cups (255 g) cooked chickpeas

2 eggs, beaten

1 cup (200 g) cooked brown rice

½ cup (30 g) panko or coarse bread crumbs, plus additional if needed

2 tablespoons roughly chopped fresh parsley (optional)

¼ teaspoon freshly ground black pepper

1. Preheat the oven to 375°F (190°C).

2. Toss the zucchini and ½ teaspoon of the salt in a colander and let stand for 10 minutes. Squeeze out as much liquid as possible.

3. Combine the TVP and the hot water in a small bowl. Let stand for 10 minutes.

4. Heat 1 tablespoon of the oil in a medium skillet over medium heat. Add the onion and cook until it just begins to soften, about 5 minutes. Add the mushrooms and cook, stirring periodically, until softened and browned, 8 to 10 minutes. Add the tomato paste, quickly stirring to combine, then the zucchini. Cook until the zucchini is slightly softened and dried out, 3 to 5 minutes. Add the vinegar and deglaze, scraping up browned bits with a wooden spoon or spatula. Remove from the heat and allow to cool slightly.

5. In the bowl of a food processor, combine the vegetable mixture and the chickpeas and eggs. Pulse until uniformly blitzed but not completely puréed—you want the vegetables to be somewhat recognizable. Add the TVP and the rice, panko, parsley, if using, pepper, and the remaining salt, and pulse to combine. Add additional panko if needed. Shape into 6 patties.

6. To cook (see pages 23–24 for detailed cooking instructions), warm a wide skillet over medium heat, then add the remaining oil. Add as many burgers as will fit comfortably without crowding the pan (usually 3 burgers will fit into a 10-inch/ 25 cm skillet), and cook until browned and crisped on the bottom, 5 to 7 minutes, then flip and repeat on the other side. The burgers will firm up a bit as they cook, and further once they're removed from the heat and have cooled slightly. Serve warm.

Ginger-Soy Tempeh Burgers with Pineapple Ⓥ🄶🄵

Makes four 4-inch (10 cm) burgers

This is an embarrassingly simple "burger"—marinated tempeh that's fried until crisp. But paired with pineapple, it's really quite special. On a whole wheat roll, fresh, crispy toppings bring excellent texture to the assembled burger: lettuce and tomato, of course, but also sprouts and avocado slices.

Two 8-ounce (277 g) packages tempeh (GF)

4 tablespoons olive oil

¼ cup (60 ml) pineapple juice

1 tablespoon finely grated fresh ginger

2 garlic cloves, crushed and peeled

2 sprigs fresh parsley

2 tablespoons soy sauce or tamari (GF)

1 teaspoon toasted sesame oil

2 teaspoons agave nectar or 1 tablespoon honey

¼ teaspoon black pepper

4 fresh or canned pineapple rings

1. Slice the tempeh in half horizontally and cut each piece in two.

2. Bring about 1 inch (2.5 cm) water to a simmer in a saucepan. Place the tempeh in a steaming basket and set inside the saucepan, cover, and steam for 10 minutes.

3. Meanwhile, combine 3 tablespoons of the oil, the pineapple juice, ginger, garlic, parsley, soy sauce, sesame oil, agave, and pepper in a shallow baking pan. Add the tempeh, cover, and marinate for at least 1 hour, flipping every 15 minutes, or up to overnight, covered and stored in the refrigerator.

4. Heat a skillet over medium-high heat. Add the remaining oil, then arrange the tempeh squares in a single layer. Drizzle with about 1 tablespoon of the marinade. Cook until browned on the bottom, 5 to 7 minutes. Turn, drizzle with another tablespoon of the marinade, and cook until browned on the top side, 5 to 7 minutes. Remove from the pan and keep warm.

5. Return the pan to the heat, add the pineapple slices, and cook until they take on some color, 3 to 5 minutes. Serve the pineapple and the tempeh on buns.

Tofu-Mushroom Burgers Ⓥ ㉓

Makes six 4-in (10 cm) burgers

These tofu burgers utilize my favorite tofu-in-a-veggie-burger technique that both A) harnesses the binding power of puréed tofu and B) preserves the more-agreeable light and delicate texture of fresh tofu. And it's accomplished by using both the food processor and a box grater. Paired with umami-rich mushrooms, it's truly one of the "meatier" burgers out there, because it's quite protein-rich and hearty. Think of it as a bit of a template, in that you can swap in nuts like cashews or almonds for the sunflower seeds, and greens that have been cooked down and drained can be easily substituted for (or added to) the mushrooms. I love this burger topped with a slice of nicely melting cheese like cheddar or provolone as well as a pile of sautéed sliced mushrooms.

4 tablespoons olive oil

5 ounces (142 g) button or cremini mushrooms, coarsely chopped

3 garlic cloves, minced

One 14- to 16-ounce (397–454 g) block firm tofu, pressed dry

¼ cup (33 g) toasted, hulled sunflower seeds

2 teaspoons potato starch, cornstarch, or arrowroot starch

1 scallion, green and white parts, thinly sliced

1 tablespoon soy sauce

¼ cup (15 g) panko or coarse bread crumbs (optional)

1. Warm 2 tablespoons of the oil in a wide skillet over medium heat, then add the mushrooms. Cook until they release their liquid and it cooks off, 6 to 8 minutes. Stir in the garlic and cook until fragrant, about 1 minute, and remove from the heat. Allow to cool briefly.

2. Break off about one third of the tofu and add it to the bowl of a food processor, along with the sunflower seeds and potato starch. Purée until the mixture is smooth and tacky. Add the mushrooms and the scallion and soy sauce, then pulse a few times to combine. Transfer this mixture to a mixing bowl.

3. Using the large holes of a box grater, grate the remaining two thirds of the tofu and add it to the puréed mixture, along with the panko, if using. Fold in until the mixture coheres, then shape into 6 burgers.

4. To cook (see pages 23–24 for detailed cooking instructions), warm a wide skillet over medium heat, then add the remaining oil. Add as many burgers as will fit comfortably without crowding the pan (usually 3 burgers will fit into a 10-inch/25 cm skillet), and cook until browned and crisped on the bottom, 3 to 5 minutes, then flip and repeat on the other side. The burgers will firm up a bit as they cook, and further once they're removed from the heat and have cooled slightly. Serve warm.

Burger Buns

Decent burger buns are available at all manner of grocery stores and bakeries, but it is a worthwhile treat (and perhaps a fun challenge) to make your own. If you don't own a stand mixer, don't let that stop you from trying out any of these recipes. Bread has been around far, far longer than our precious KitchenAids. In fact, I often find that making breads and burger buns by hand gives me a better feel for the dough and results in a better outcome. Here are some guidelines.

✳ **A WETTER DOUGH WILL BE LESS DENSE:** This realization, late in my life as a baker, shattered my approach to bread-making. I imagine that many of us who grew up helping make bread were told that we should be liberal with flour and then just knead, knead, knead, until the dough is "smooth and elastic." News flash: If you add too much flour, it will never get "smooth and elastic." One should, in fact, opt for a wetter dough and resist the urge to add additional flour during kneading; a dough that might stick a bit to your hands and the work surface will make better bread. This is one reason I've come to prefer making bread by hand to using a stand mixer. With the stand mixer, it's difficult to resist adding more flour as it sticks to the bowl and the dough hook.

To knead a slightly sticky dough, knead with one hand and hold a dough scraper in the other. Use the scraper to get underneath the dough and flip it after each kneading.

✳ **WHEN USING A STAND MIXER:** If you do opt to use the stand mixer, here are a few guidelines. Start with the paddle attachment, which will ensure that the base dough is thoroughly combined. After about 2 minutes, switch to the dough hook. Add as much flour as is needed for the dough to form a ball. As the dough kneads, periodically turn off the mixer and remove the dough from the hook with your hands so that all the dough gets uniformly kneaded. I recommend kneading by hand for the final few minutes, if for no other reason than posterity's sake.

✳ **COMBINING FLOURS:** Breads and rolls that are not made entirely from all-purpose white flour have a more nuanced flavor and an enhanced nutritional profile. I prefer that half the flour be unbleached all-purpose white flour or bread flour and the other half a combination of whole wheat or spelt. Other types of flour—rye, buckwheat, oat—can be incorporated, but I don't advise using any more than 25 percent of the total flour volume. Due to the higher volume of perishable oils they contain, whole grain flours are best stored in the refrigerator or freezer in an airtight container, where they will stay fresh for months.

✳ **A NOTE ABOUT GLUTEN-FREE ROLLS:** Gluten-free bread-baking is a skill set of its own, and practitioners of the craft have come a long way since the first edition of this book was released in 2010. In that first edition, I included a recipe for gluten-free sandwich "bread," using a packaged mix and cooking it in a square pan, then slicing it like focaccia and splitting each piece in half for burgers. This is still a great way to go, but since that's such a simple alternative, I don't think it merits a recipe, so it no longer appears here. More importantly, I encourage you to seek out the skilled GF bakers in your hometown to support.

SHAPING ROLLS

If you have a scale, divide the dough (which has been risen once) into 3-ounce portions. This is roughly the size of a large plum (fig. 1). Place a portion of dough on an unfloured surface. Place your dominant hand loosely, like a cage, around the dough with your fingers touching the surface of the table or countertop, then swirl the dough against the table in a circle (fig. 2). It should only take 10 to 15 seconds; the friction against the work surface causes the dough to collect at the base and shape itself into a ball (fig. 3).

Basic Burger Buns

Makes 10 buns

Here's a simple recipe for homemade hamburger buns, one where nondairy milk works beautifully. They're rich and moist and good enough to serve as dinner rolls. But as buns for veggie burgers, they're best toasted before assembling. Feel free to use only all-purpose flour here, or another flour for the oat flour.

1 cup (240 ml) warm milk or rice milk (110°F to 115°F/ 43–46°C)

½ cup (120 ml) warm water (110°F to 115°F/43–46°C)

1 tablespoon honey or maple syrup

2¼ teaspoons active dry yeast (1 package)

¼ cup (60 ml) olive oil, plus more for the dough bowl

1½ to 2½ cups (180–300 g) all-purpose flour

1 cup (113 g) whole wheat flour

½ cup (45 g) oat flour

2½ teaspoons salt

Egg wash: 1 beaten egg plus 1 tablespoon whole milk, or 2 tablespoons soy milk plus ½ teaspoon cornstarch

Poppy seeds, sesame seeds, wheat bran, flax seeds, or any combination

1. In a small bowl, stir together the milk, water, and honey. Whisk in the yeast and let stand for about 5 minutes, until the yeast begins to foam. Whisk in the oil.

2. In a large bowl, whisk 1 cup (120 g) of the all-purpose flour with the whole wheat flour, oat flour, and salt, then stir in the yeast mixture.

3. To mix by hand, stir with a wooden spoon until thoroughly combined, adding more flour as needed, until it shapes into a ball. Turn the dough onto a floured surface and knead until smooth and elastic, 10 to 12 minutes, judiciously adding more flour as needed. Loosely shape the dough into a round.

4. To use the standing mixer, begin with the paddle attachment, stirring the dough until combined, 2 minutes. Switch to the dough hook and knead until smooth and elastic, 8 to 10 minutes, judiciously adding more flour as needed. Loosely shape the dough into a round.

5. Pour about 1 teaspoon oil into the mixing bowl and coat the dough with it. Cover with a piece of plastic wrap or a large tea cloth and let stand in a warm place until doubled in size, 1 to 2 hours.

6. Turn the dough onto a work surface and shape into 10 rolls (see page 109).

7. Line a baking sheet with parchment paper. Space the rolls 3 to 4 inches (7.5–10 cm) apart on the baking sheet. Cover again with plastic wrap or a tea towel. Let stand in a warm place until doubled in size, 1 to 2 hours, or allow to rise overnight in the refrigerator.

8. Preheat the oven to 400°F (200°C).

9. Brush the buns with the egg wash and sprinkle with the seed garnish, being sure to cover the bun as much as possible. Bake for 15 to 18 minutes, turning the pan halfway through. Flip a roll over to check that it is browned on the base, which will indicate its doneness. Cool completely.

Whole Wheat Burger Buns

Makes 10 buns

These buns have the perfect burger bun texture: a crispy crust that yields to the soft goodness inside. The molasses gives them a slightly musky flavor and a dark brown color. I'm happy to eat them without anything sandwiched inside. To make these buns vegan, use your favorite unflavored nondairy milk and simply omit the egg. They'll be a bit less rich but still very good.

1 cup (240 ml) warm water (110°F to 115°F/43–46°C)

3 tablespoons warm whole milk or nondairy milk (110°F to 115°F/43–46°C)

2 tablespoons molasses

1 tablespoon sugar

2¼ teaspoons active dry yeast (1 package)

1½ to 2½ cups (180–300 g) bread flour

1¼ cups (141 g) whole wheat flour

2¾ teaspoons salt

2 tablespoons olive oil, plus more for the dough bowl

1 egg, beaten (see headnote)

Egg wash: 1 beaten egg plus 1 tablespoon water or milk

Poppy seeds, sesame seeds, wheat bran, flaxseeds, or any combination

1. In a small bowl, add the water, milk, molasses, and sugar, whisking to combine. Whisk in the yeast and let stand for about 5 minutes, until the yeast begins to foam.

2. In a large bowl, whisk 1 cup (120 g) of the bread flour with the whole wheat flour and salt. Stir in the yeast mixture and the oil and egg.

3. To mix by hand, stir with a wooden spoon until thoroughly combined, adding more flour as needed, until it shapes into a ball. Turn the dough onto a floured surface and knead until smooth and elastic, 10 to 12 minutes, judiciously adding more flour as needed. Loosely shape the dough into a round.

4. To use the standing mixer, begin with the paddle attachment, stirring the dough until combined, 2 minutes. Switch to the dough hook and knead until smooth and elastic, 8 to 10 minutes, judiciously adding more flour as needed. Loosely shape the dough into a round.

5. Pour about 1 teaspoon oil into the mixing bowl and coat the dough with it. Cover with a piece of plastic wrap or a large tea cloth and let stand in a warm place until doubled in size, 1 to 2 hours.

6. Turn the dough onto a work surface and shape into 10 rolls (see page 109).

7. Line a baking sheet with parchment paper. Space the rolls 3 to 4 inches (7.5–10 cm) apart on the baking sheet. Cover again with plastic wrap or a tea towel. Let stand in a warm place until doubled in size, 1 to 2 hours, or allow to rise overnight in the refrigerator.

8. Preheat the oven to 400°F (200°C).

9. Brush the buns with the egg wash and sprinkle with the seed garnish, being sure to cover the buns as much as possible. Bake for 15 minutes, turning the pan halfway through. Flip a roll over to check that it is browned on the base, which will indicate its doneness. Cool completely.

Pretzel Rolls

Makes 12 rolls

Though pretzel rolls are a minor ordeal and a mess to make, they are a true indulgence right out of the oven—one hand for the roll, the other for the squeeze bottle of mustard. They're also delicious with hearty veggie burgers like the Seitan Burgers with Mango BBQ Sauce (page 98) and the Butternut Squash and Black Bean Burgers (page 76).

¾ cup (180 ml) warm whole milk or nondairy milk (110°F to 115°F/43–46°C)

¾ cup (180 ml) warm water (110°F to 115°F/43–46°C)

2¼ teaspoons active dry yeast (1 package)

3 tablespoons olive oil, plus more for the dough bowl

3 to 3½ cups (360–420 g) bread flour

1 teaspoon plus 1 tablespoon salt

¼ cup (58 g) baking soda

Rock salt, for sprinkling, or additional salt

1. Combine the milk and water in a large bowl. Stir in the yeast and let stand for 5 minutes, until it bubbles and foams. Add the oil, 2½ cups (300 g) of the flour, and 1 teaspoon of the salt.

2. To mix by hand, stir with a wooden spoon until thoroughly combined, adding more flour as needed, until it shapes into a ball. Turn the dough onto a floured surface and knead until smooth and elastic, 10 to 12 minutes, judiciously adding more flour as needed. Loosely shape the dough into a round.

3. To use the standing mixer, begin with the paddle attachment, stirring the dough until combined, 2 minutes. Switch to the dough hook and knead until smooth and elastic, 8 to 10 minutes, judiciously adding more flour as needed. Loosely shape the dough into a round.

4. Pour about 1 teaspoon oil into the mixing bowl and coat the dough with it. Cover with a piece of plastic wrap or a large tea cloth and let stand in a warm place until doubled in size, 1 to 2 hours.

5. Turn the dough onto a work surface and shape into 12 rolls (see page 109).

6. Line a baking sheet with parchment paper. Space the rolls 3 to 4 inches (7.5–10 cm) apart on the baking sheet. Cover again with plastic wrap or a tea towel. Let stand in a warm place until doubled in size, 1 to 2 hours, or allow to rise overnight in the refrigerator.

7. Preheat the oven to 400°F (200°C).

8. Fill a large pot with 4 to 5 inches (10–13 cm) water and bring to a boil. Carefully add the baking soda (it will foam up) and the remaining salt.

9. After the rolls have risen a second time, add them to the boiling water in batches of 4 and poach 1 minute per side.

10. Place the poached rolls 1 inch (2.5 cm) apart on the baking sheet. With a sharp knife, draw an "X" on the top of each roll and sprinkle with the rock salt. Bake for 15 to 20 minutes, until dark brown all over. Transfer to a cooling rack. Cool completely.

Corn Bread Buns

Makes 10 buns

Yeasted corn bread is a delicious alternative to corn bread that's leavened with baking soda or baking powder. It has a softer, spongier texture. Cornmeal is a heavier grain than flour, however, so the trick to getting these buns right is not to overdo it with the flours. Additionally, these are more robust in flavor and texture than traditional hamburger buns, so they need to be paired with equally robust burgers, such as Sweet Potato Burgers with Lentils and Kale (page 82) or Best Portobello Burgers (page 62), and they're also great with the Seitan Burgers with Mango BBQ Sauce (page 98).

½ cup (120 ml) warm milk (110°F to 115°F/ 43–46°C)

½ cup (120 ml) warm water (110°F to 115°F/43–46°C)

2¼ teaspoons active dry yeast (1 package)

¼ cup (60 ml) olive oil, plus more for the dough bowl

¼ cup (85 g) honey or maple syrup

2 eggs

1 to 2 cups (120–240 g) all-purpose flour

1 cup (113 g) whole wheat flour

1 cup cornmeal (156 g), plus more for sprinkling

2 teaspoons teaspoon salt

Egg wash: 1 beaten egg plus 1 tablespoon water or milk

Fleur de sel, for sprinkling

1. Whisk together the milk and water, then stir in the yeast. Let stand for about 5 minutes, until the yeast begins to foam. Whisk in the oil, honey, and eggs.

2. In a large bowl, whisk 1 cup (120 g) of the all-purpose flour with the whole wheat flour, cornmeal, and salt. Add the yeast mixture.

3. To mix by hand, stir with a wooden spoon until thoroughly combined, adding more flour as needed, until it shapes into a ball. Turn the dough onto a floured surface and knead until smooth and elastic, 10 to 12 minutes, judiciously adding more flour as needed. Loosely shape the dough into a round.

4. To use the standing mixer, begin with the paddle attachment, stirring the dough until combined, 2 minutes. Switch to the dough hook and knead until smooth and elastic, 8 to 10 minutes, judiciously adding more flour as needed. Loosely shape the mixture into a round.

5. Pour about 1 teaspoon oil into the mixing bowl and coat the dough with it. Cover with a piece of plastic wrap or a large tea cloth and let stand in a warm place until doubled in size, 1 to 2 hours.

6. Turn the dough onto a work surface and shape into 10 rolls (see page 109).

7. Line a baking sheet with parchment paper. Space the rolls 3 to 4 inches (7.5–10 cm) apart on the baking sheet. Cover again with plastic wrap or a tea towel. Let stand in a warm place until doubled in size, 1 to 2 hours, or allow to rise overnight in the refrigerator.

8. Preheat the oven to 400°F (200°C).

9. Brush the buns with the egg wash and sprinkle with fleur de sel and a bit of cornmeal. Bake for 12 to 15 minutes, turning the pan halfway through. Flip a roll over to check that it is browned on the base, which will indicate its doneness. Cool completely.

ALTERNATIVES TO BUNS: OTHER WAYS TO SERVE VEGGIE BURGERS

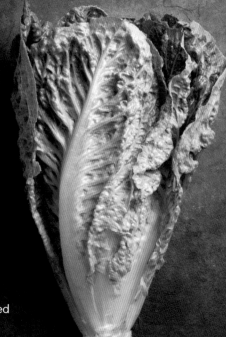

All my preaching in this chapter aside, there is no rule stating that veggie burgers must be served on burger buns. Thinking of your veggie burger mix as the ground "meat," there's also no reason you can't shape them into something other than a big burger—this, after all, is something that was at the heart of my Made by Lukas burger business. Here are a few of my favorite alternatives.

* **PITA BREAD:** Split pita in half and gently pry open, then stuff with your favorite veggie burger and toppings.

* **LETTUCE CUPS:** Use sturdy, crisp lettuce, like Bibb lettuce or romaine hearts. Less-crisp lettuce can always be wrapped around the burgers and filling, too.

* **SANDWICH BREAD:** Add a veggie burger in a veggie patty melt, toasting the bread and serving it with your favorite cheese. Leftover cold or room-temperature burgers also go great with your favorite sandwich toppings.

* **FRIED VEGGIE BURGER "FALAFEL":** Scoop the burger mix into 2-tablespoon-size potions and shape into balls. Deep-fry them by submerging in 2 inches (5 cm) of hot vegetable oil, maintained at a temperature of 375°F (190°C).

* **WRAPS:** Cut your burger in half and arrange over a large tortilla, along with whatever other fillings you prefer, then roll up and serve.

* **OVER SALAD:** One of my favorite veggie burger serving methods—add a large burger or a few smaller sliders to your favorite green or grain-based salad.

* **AS SLIDERS, WITH DIP:** Smaller-portioned warm or room-temperature veggie burger sliders are a great appetizer or snack. Serve with your favorite dip, such as a yogurt-based one.

* **CRUMBLED AND STIR-FRIED:** Leftover burgers can be crumbled into a hot pan and stir-fried with your favorite taco seasonings or vegetable medley. Alternatively, leftover veggie burger mix can be "scrambled" in hot pan, then turned into a meal with a medley of other veggies.

* **BAKED "MEATBALLS":** This works best with drier, easier-to-shape burgers like the Tofu-Mushroom Burgers (page 104), Kale and Quinoa Burgers (page 42), or Carrot-Parsnip Burgers with Almonds (page 73). Shape into balls, then bake in the oven at 375°F (190°C) for 15 to 20 minutes, until firmed. Serve with your favorite tomato sauce.

* **BREAKFAST "SAUSAGES":** Portion about 2 tablespoons each, then cook in a hot skillet, and cook them "Smash Burger" style. Serve with fried eggs or scrambled tofu.

* **BURGER AS BUN:** This is a genius method from Heidi Swanson, of *101 Cookbooks* and the Super Natural cookbook series. Split your veggie burgers in half as you would a layer cake, and treat the burger itself as a bun, with your favorite toppings inside.

Sides: Salads and Fries

One of the many pioneering aspects of vegetarian and vegan cooking is the rethinking of how a "proper" meal is supposed to be laid out. Growing up, I was taught that a meal was a big ol' hunk of meat taking up most of the plate, adorned with small amounts of starches and vegetables nudged up against the rim.

Vegetarian and vegan eating has demonstrated, for me at least, that no one thing needs to necessarily be the star of the show, and that every aspect of the meal is equally important—whether it's salad, soup, side, or veggie burger. The sense of balance need not skew in one direction or another, and nothing needs to play second fiddle to anything else. To this end, I like to think of all the salads in this chapter as "mains"—even if they are "light" mains—rather than as secondary accompaniments.

That said, salads are extremely versatile dishes, and they don't have to be fussy. The best sides and salads, in my opinion, are often the simplest. Here are some suggestions for quick burger accompaniments if you are pressed for time.

* **A plate of thickly sliced ripe tomatoes sprinkled with salt and pepper**

* **Quartered roasted beets, sprinkled with wine vinegar and drizzled with olive oil**

* **Fresh arugula tossed with lemon zest and a simple vinaigrette**

* **Small zucchini, blistered over the flames on a grill or under a broiler, coarsely chopped and sprinkled with herbs and olive oil**

* **Sliced, quartered, or cubed radishes tossed with salt, rice vinegar, and chile flakes**

* **A plate of crudités: florets of cauliflower and broccoli, asparagus spears, green beans, jicama slices, cherry tomatoes, and quartered cooked red bliss potatoes**

But what would a burger cookbook be without fries? I offer a few different takes on oven-baked french fries (plus, I've included some guidelines for deep-frying for those special occasions when it's called for).

Watermelon and Citrus Salad Ⓥ Ⓖⓕ

Makes 4 servings

Make this salad when watermelon is at its peak, sugar-sweet and juicy. I prefer basil to the fresh mint typically used in watermelon salad, but feel free to use mint instead.

VINAIGRETTE

¼ cup (60 ml) fresh orange juice

Juice of 1 lime

1 tablespoon red or white wine vinegar

1 shallot, sliced into rings

¼ teaspoon salt

¼ teaspoon ground white pepper

SALAD

2 oranges

6 cups (912 g) watermelon, cut into 1-inch (2.5 cm) cubes

¾ cup (20 g) thinly sliced fresh basil

½ cup (50 g) toasted sliced or slivered almonds

½ cup (75 g) crumbled feta cheese (optional)

Olive oil, for serving

1. To make the vinaigrette, combine the orange juice, lime juice, vinegar, shallot, salt, and pepper in a small bowl or jar. Let stand for 10 minutes.

2. To make the salad, slice off the top and bottom ends of the oranges and place the flat bottom on a cutting board. With a sharp chef's knife, cut off the peel in strips all the way around the orange, following the curve of the fruit. Slice the oranges into ¼-inch-thick (6 mm) rounds.

3. Arrange the orange slices and the watermelon over a platter, then drizzle with the vinaigrette. Just before serving, garnish with the basil, almonds, and feta cheese, if using, and drizzle with olive oil.

DO AHEAD: Cube watermelon, prepare vinaigrette

Roasted Carrot Salad with Chickpeas and Dates Ⓥ ⒼⒻ

Makes 4 to 6 servings

This is a sweet fall salad, in which roasted carrots become nearly candied and then are pushed even further in that direction by pairing with dates and oranges. A bracing vinaigrette plus crunchy, quenching fennel, and earthy chickpeas prevents the salad from becoming cloying. Different colored carrots make this salad even more striking, and when I buy fresh, juicy organic ones, I never bother to peel them. It's a good "make ahead" salad in that it keeps well when transported to picnics and cookouts—the fennel softens, and the flavors meld.

1 pound (454 g) carrots, peeled if desired

4 tablespoons olive oil

1 tablespoon plus ½ teaspoon honey

2 tablespoons apple cider vinegar

¾ teaspoon salt, plus additional salt as needed

1 small bulb fennel, fonds reserved

1 orange

1 tablespoon fresh lemon juice

½ teaspoon ground cumin

Freshly ground black pepper

One 15-ounce (425 g) can chickpeas, drained and rinsed

4 dates, coarsely chopped

1. Preheat the oven to 425°F (220°C). Line a baking sheet with parchment paper or aluminum foil.

2. Slice the carrots into coins about ¼ inch (6 mm) thick. In a mixing bowl, whisk together 2 tablespoons of the olive oil, 1 tablespoon of the honey, 1 tablespoon of the vinegar, and ½ teaspoon of the salt, until combined. Add the carrots, toss to combine, then spread them out on the prepared baking sheet. Transfer to the oven and roast for 20 to 25 minutes, until tender and caramelized. Allow to cool.

3. Slice the fennel in half through the core, then trim out the core. With the cut sides down, slice the white part of the bulb into very thin ribbons. Compost the green stalks or reserve for another use.

4. Trim off the peel of the orange and slice into thin rings, then quarters, or supreme the orange by holding the peeled fruit in your hand and carefully trimming the fruit from the membranes.

5. In a small jar, combine the lemon juice with the remaining oil, vinegar, honey, and salt, and the cumin and pepper. Seal and shake until combined. (Alternatively, whisk the ingredients together in a small bowl.)

6. To serve, combine the carrots, fennel, and orange and the chickpeas, dates, and dressing to taste in a serving bowl and toss until combined. Garnish with the fennel fronds and serve.

Red Cabbage Slaw ⓖⓕ

Makes 4 servings

I made this salad when my friend Ilsa Jule invited me up to her farm, back when she used to have it in Western Massachusetts, and I used basically every vegetable I could get my hands on—a handful of thinly sliced fennel and fronds, some basil, grated carrots, and radishes. It was a fortifying, refreshing lunch in itself. The recipe below is a delicious simplification of that salad. Feel free to improvise. If you can't find the thicker Greek-style yogurt, see page 165 for instructions on how to drain regular yogurt.

½ **head red cabbage**

1 tablespoon rice wine vinegar

½ **teaspoon salt**

Freshly ground black pepper

3 tablespoons plain Greek-style yogurt

¼ **cup (2 g) coarsely chopped fresh dill**

Freshly ground black pepper

1. To julienne the cabbage, quarter it along the core and trim out the cores. Slice the cabbage as thinly as possible—about ⅛-inch-thick (3 mm) slices. Alternatively, shave the cabbage using a mandoline.

2. Toss the cabbage with the vinegar and salt in a large bowl and let stand until the cabbage begins to wilt, 10 to 15 minutes. Pour off any liquid that has collected at the bottom of the bowl. Add the yogurt, dill, and pepper. Adjust seasonings. Serve.

VARIATION: Asian-Style Slaw

Omit the yogurt and substitute the following dressing:
2 tablespoons soy sauce, 1 tablespoon honey, 1 teaspoon toasted sesame oil, 1 tablespoon toasted sesame seeds, and a few sliced scallions.

Roasted Corn Salad Ⓥ ⒼⒻ

Makes 6 servings

When corn is fresh, in season, and juicy, it doesn't even need to be cooked—simply slice it off the ears and eat right away. But when it's less fresh, boiling it cooks the starches in the kernels and makes the corn sweeter. This salad hopes you've got seasonal corn, but if not, just plunge it into a pot of boiling water for about 3 minutes, which will ensure its finished texture is juicy. Lastly, everything here can be cooked on the grill if you'd like to add some smoky notes. Heat the oil in a skillet directly on the grill, then add the peppers and corn and cook until tender.

¼ cup (60 ml) olive oil

3 cups (495 g) fresh corn kernels

2 jalapeños, minced (seeded or not, depending on your personal heat threshold)

Juice of 1 lime

1 shallot, minced

Salt

Freshly ground black pepper

½ cup (75 g) crumbled feta or cotija cheese (optional)

1. Preheat the oven to 350°F (180°C).

2. Heat the oil in an oven-safe skillet or sauté pan over medium heat. Add the corn and jalapeños, tossing quickly to combine. Transfer the pan to the oven and roast, stirring occasionally, for 15 to 20 minutes, until the corn is tender. Allow to cool to room temperature.

3. In a large bowl, toss the corn and jalapeños with the lime juice, shallot, and salt and pepper to taste. Serve hot, chilled, or at room temperature, garnished with the cheese, if using.

Grilled Summer Salad with Creamy Sunflower Dressing ⓥ ⓖⓕ

Makes 4 to 6 servings

While this salad is all about the dressing, to me, it also illustrates what a versatile, not-boring ingredient lettuce can be. Briefly grilling it allows new flavors to appear, slightly softening the vegetable and creating an altogether new salad experience. But back to the dressing: It does require a high-speed blender to achieve the creaminess that makes it so delicious and exciting. Sunflower seeds lend a nutty depth, and charred zucchini provides body and a mild, charred-tasting neutral base. The rest of the ingredients provide personality. It makes a great dip for crudites and chips, too.

DRESSING

¼ cup (33 g) hulled sunflower seeds

1 small or ½ medium zucchini

2 tablespoons olive oil, plus more for brushing

1 serrano chile, seeded

1 small bunch cilantro, stems and leaves

¼ teaspoon salt

2 teaspoons miso paste

1 to 2 tablespoons fresh lemon juice

SALAD

1 large or 2 small heads romaine or other crunchy lettuce

2 ears corn, shucked

½ cup (75 g) cherry tomatoes, halved

1 serrano chile, very thinly sliced

1. To make the dressing, cover the sunflower seeds with hot tap water and set aside for 20 minutes, until softened through. Drain and rinse.

2. Meanwhile, char the zucchini. Prepare a medium-high flame and preheat your grill. When hot, place the zucchini directly over the flames and cook, turning periodically, until blackened all over and the zucchini is tender, which will take anywhere from 10 to 12 minutes. (No need to trim your zucchini or rub it with olive oil.) If you don't have access to a grill, you can use this same method by cooking the zucchini over a gas burner or under the broiler, close to the heat source.

3. Combine the rinsed sunflower seeds and charred zucchini with the olive oil, chile, cilantro, salt, and miso in a high-speed blender and process until very smooth. Add the lemon juice, starting with half to taste, and adding more as needed.

4. Slice the romaine into quarters through the core(s), so that each piece holds together.

5. Brush the corn lightly with oil. On the prepared grill, place the corn over the flame and grill, turning periodically, until lightly charred all over, which will take about 5 minutes. Allow to cool, then slice the kernels off with a sharp chef's knife by holding each ear upright on a cutting board and slicing downward, turning the corn as you go.

6. At the same time, arrange the romaine over the flame and cook for 1 to 2 minutes per side, until lightly charred on the cut sides. Coarsely chop the romaine and arrange over a serving platter.

7. To serve, drizzle the dressing over the lettuce to taste, then scatter the corn, tomatoes, and chile on top. Serve warm or at room temperature.

Raw Kale Salad with Apples and Candied Walnuts Ⓥ ⒼⒻ

Makes 6 servings

I like this salad in the late fall, just when I begin to prepare myself for the oncoming winter and its dearth of fresh fruits and vegetables. It's delicious alongside almost any veggie burger, though the Sweet Potato Burgers with Lentils and Kale (page 82) and the Red Lentil and Celeriac Burgers (page 52) are most perfect matches.

2 tablespoons sugar

¼ cup (25 g) toasted walnuts, coarsely chopped

Pinch of dried thyme

Pinch of cayenne pepper

2 tablespoons soy sauce or tamari (GF)

1 tablespoon lemon juice

2 teaspoons honey or 1½ teaspoons agave nectar

1 teaspoon toasted sesame oil

¼ cup (60 ml) olive oil

1 bunch kale, cleaned and trimmed of stalks, and chopped or torn into ½- to 1-inch (1.25–2.5 cm) pieces

1 medium apple (a sweet and crisp one like Gala), cut into thin slices

½ cup (78 g) shredded celeriac

1. To candy the walnuts, heat a dry, heavy-bottomed skillet over medium-low heat. Pour in the sugar and swirl the pan to distribute the sugar evenly. Cook, swirling the pan occasionally as the sugar begins to melt and brown. When it is a dark amber color, after 8 to 10 minutes, remove from the heat. Working quickly, before the sugar seizes up, add the walnuts, thyme, and cayenne, stirring so that everything is evenly coated. Transfer the mixture to a plate to cool, then break into small pieces.

2. To make the dressing, in a small bowl, combine the soy sauce, lemon juice, and honey. Whisk in the sesame oil in a steady stream. Adjust seasonings.

3. In a large serving bowl, combine the walnuts and the kale, apple, and celeriac. Toss with the dressing just before serving.

DO AHEAD: Caramelize walnuts

Beet, Pickle, and Apple Salad Ⓥ ⓖⓕ

Makes 4 servings

The trick to this embarrassingly simple salad is to use the right apple: it must be snappily crisp and tart. If its grainy or soft, the whole salad will be off. This is an excellent use of leftover roasted beets. Know that the longer it sits, the more purple the salad will become.

2 medium red or golden beets, scrubbed clean and trimmed of stems and fibrous roots

1 teaspoon olive oil

2 apples, such as Granny Smith or Cortland, peeled and cut into ¼-inch (6 mm) die

1 cup (240 ml) Quick Pickles (page 151), cut into ¼-inch (6 mm) die

¼ cup (15 g) coarsely chopped fresh mint

Freshly ground black pepper

1. To roast the beets, preheat the oven to 400°F (200°C). Place the beets on a square of aluminum foil and rub with the oil. Wrap tightly in the foil and roast for 45 minutes to 1 hour, until they can be effortlessly pierced with a knife or skewer. Allow to cool completely. When safe to handle, peel the beets and cut into ¼-inch (6 mm) dice.

2. Gently mix the beets with the apples, pickles, mint, and pepper to taste. Serve cold or at room temperature.

DO AHEAD: Roast the beets

Black Olive and Roasted Potato Salad with Arugula Ⓥ ⒼⒻ

Makes 4 servings

I love a potato salad that is not mayo-based. The lemon, sherry vinegar, and arugula offset the briny-ness of the olive tapenade in this recipe. Feel free to substitute any variety of white potato you have lying around, but including the sweet potato is crucial. If you don't have the time or inclination to make your own olive tapenade, simply use ½ cup (135 g) of store-bought olive tapenade in place of the olives puréed in step 2 below.

½ cup (60 g) pitted kalamata olives (see headnote)

1 sweet potato

6 fingerling potatoes or 1 large Yukon gold potato

1 Red Bliss potato

4 tablespoons olive oil

Juice of ½ lemon

1 tablespoon sherry vinegar

¼ teaspoon salt

½ red onion, halved and sliced into half-rings

3 cups (60 g) loosely packed baby arugula

Freshly ground black pepper

1. Preheat the oven to 400°F (200°C).

2. To make the tapenade, use a blender, mini food processor, or handheld immersion blender to purée the olives until smooth. If you have a mortar and pestle, that'll also work—it'll just take a bit longer.

3. Cut the potatoes into uniform 1-inch (2.5 cm) pieces (it's not necessary to peel them). Toss with 2 tablespoons of the tapenade and 2 tablespoons of the oil. Spread out on a baking sheet and roast for 30 to 35 minutes, until cooked through. Allow to cool.

4. In a large mixing bowl, whisk the remaining tapenade and the remaining oil with the lemon juice, vinegar, and salt. Add the onion and let stand for 10 minutes. Add the potatoes and the arugula and toss. Season with pepper and serve immediately.

DO AHEAD: Roast potatoes, make dressing

Barley Salad with Beets and Goat Cheese

Makes 4 servings

This salad is the everyday version of the sensational Warm Farro Salad at Al Di La Trattoria in Brooklyn. While not crucial at all, it's delicious if you can pull off serving it warm. Here's how: Have everything ready to go—cook the beets and toast the hazelnuts, mix the dressing, have the cheese at room temperature—so that while the barley is still warm, you can rush it to the dinner table. Well-toasted hazelnuts also deliver a lot of flavor—toast them in an oven preheated to 325°F (165°C) until a halved nut is chestnut-colored all the way through, for 12 to 15 minutes or more. Then use a clean paper or kitchen towel to rub the skins off.

2 medium beets, scrubbed clean and trimmed of stems and fibrous roots

3 tablespoons plus 1 teaspoon good-quality olive oil

¾ cup (150 g) barley, rinsed

2 teaspoons sherry vinegar

½ teaspoon salt

Freshly ground black pepper

½ cup (55 g) hazelnuts, toasted and coarsely chopped

2 tablespoons roughly chopped fresh tarragon, plus sprigs for garnish

4 ounces (113 g) good-quality goat cheese

1. To roast the beets, preheat the oven to 400°F (200°C). Place the beets on a square of aluminum foil and rub with the 1 teaspoon oil. Cup the sides of the foil around the beets and add 1 tablespoon water, then wrap tightly in the foil and transfer to a baking sheet. Roast for 45 minutes to 1 hour, until completely tender. Allow to cool until safe to handle, then peel the beets, slice, and cut each slice into quarters—approximately ⅛ inch (3 mm).

2. To cook the barley, bring a large pot of salted water to boil. Add the barley and cook for 20 to 25 minutes, until tender. Drain and return to the pot. Toss with the vinegar. Cover the pot until ready to assemble the salad (this will keep the barley warm).

3. Whisk together the remaining oil and the salt and pepper. Toss with the barley and then the hazelnuts and tarragon. Adjust seasonings.

4. Divide the barley evenly among 4 salad plates, topping each with the beets, the goat cheese, and a sprig of tarragon.

DO AHEAD: Roast beets, toast hazelnuts

Classic Baked Fries V GF

Makes 4 servings

I wasn't a fan of baked french fries until I figured out this way to make them. It always seemed that the texture was wrong—overcooked on the outside, and dry and starchy like cotton on the inside. In this simple recipe, the combination of soaking the potatoes (which helps rid them of some excess starch), and then baking under a high heat solves the problem of texture, while keeping the salty, crispy, potato flavor going strong. French fries can be fun to sprinkle with fresh herbs, citrus zest, dried chile—really anything you please. I've added a few suggestions below for taking the seasoning in a different direction.

3 large russet potatoes

3 tablespoons canola, vegetable, or grapeseed oil, plus additional for greasing

1 teaspoon salt

1. Cut the potatoes into ¼-inch (6 mm) matchsticks (see page 139). Cover with cold water in a large bowl and let stand for 30 minutes, or up to 12 hours in the refrigerator. When ready to cook, drain and rinse the fries, then dry them thoroughly by blotting with a towel.

2. Preheat the oven to 450°F (230°C). Lightly oil a large baking sheet.

3. Toss the potatoes with the oil and salt. Spread the potatoes on the prepared baking sheet. Bake, flipping every 10 minutes, for 30 to 40 minutes, until golden and crisp. Remove with a metal spatula and toss with additional salt to taste.

VARIATIONS

Add different dried spices with the oil and salt before roasting the fries. Possibilities are endless, but here are a few suggestions.

- 1 teaspoon smoked paprika

- 1 teaspoon dried parsley, ½ teaspoon freshly ground black pepper, and ½ teaspoon dried oregano

- 1 teaspoon ground cumin and 1 teaspoon hot or mild curry powder; after roasting, toss with 2 tablespoons chopped fresh cilantro

DO AHEAD: Cut potatoes into matchsticks

CUTTING POTATOES INTO FRENCH FRIES

Make a single slice along the length of the potato so that it will stand flat on a cutting board (fig. 1).

Carefully slice lengthwise into broad, ¼-inch-thick (6 mm) disks (fig. 2).

Arrange 2 or 3 disks on top of each other and slice lengthwise into ¼-inch matchsticks (fig. 3).

TIPS

- Use a large, sturdy, sharp knife so that the knife, rather than your own elbow grease, will be doing the slicing.

- Give yourself plenty of room on a large cutting board that won't slip around the countertop. Place a moist washcloth beneath the cutting board if yours is squiggling around.

Cumin-Spiked Roasted Sweet Potato Fries Ⓥ ⒼⒻ

Makes 4 servings

I've found that the secret to making crispy fries from sweet potatoes and other root vegetables—those that are less starchy than Russet potatoes—is to add a bit of starch to their coatings, which gives them a completely delicious, slightly craggy crust. My go-to is potato starch, which is tossed with the potatoes before the olive oil and salt. These fries are delicious dipped in Mango BBQ Sauce (page 159) or Almond Yogurt Sauce (page 162). Omit the garam masala and cumin if you prefer basic sweet potato fries.

3 tablespoons olive oil, plus more for greasing

3 large sweet potatoes

2 teaspoons potato starch or cornstarch

1½ teaspoons garam masala

1 teaspoon ground cumin

1 teaspoon salt

1. Preheat the oven to 450°F (230°C). Lightly oil a large baking sheet.

2. Scrub the potatoes clean and let dry. Cut into ¼-inch (6 mm) matchsticks (see page 139).

3. Combine the potato starch, garam masala, and cumin, and toss with the potatoes. Add the oil and salt and toss.

4. Spread the potatoes on the prepared baking sheet. Bake, flipping twice, for 25 to 30 minutes, until crispy on the outside and tender on the inside. Remove with a metal spatula and toss with additional salt to taste.

DO AHEAD: Cut potatoes into matchsticks and keep covered with fresh water

DEEP-FRYING

Deep-frying, which involves completely submerging food in hot oil, may not be something you want to do frequently, but it is a worthwhile extra step for celebrations and special occasions.

To deep-fry, heat at least 4 inches of vegetable, peanut, or canola oil in a deep saucepan to 375°F (190°C). (Alternatively, heat the oil in a FryDaddy, or a wok, which is an excellent vessel for smaller-batch deep-frying projects.) In batches, carefully lower the matchstick potatoes into the oil using a heat-safe slotted spoon or tongs. Avoid crowding the pan. Cook, stirring occasionally, for 8 to 10 minutes, maintaining the temperature, until the fries are golden brown. Line a baking sheet with paper towel and transfer with a slotted spoon to drain off excess oil. Salt liberally, and serve immediately.

The oil can be cooled, strained, bottled, and reused for your next 3 or 4 deep-frying adventures. Be sure to dispose of it in accordance with your city's requirements—it should never be dumped down your sink's (or any other) drain. For information about correct disposal in your city, contact your local department of sanitation.

Broccoli "Fries" with Honey Mustard ⒼⒻ

Makes 4 to 6 servings | Sauce makes about ¾ cup (180 ml)

There's no way you'll confuse them with french fries, but in my opinion, these are just as appealing. Trimmed to be long enough that they're easy to drag through a dip—and roasted in a hot oven to become slightly charred, taking on some crispy texture—they make an excellent side dish for any kind of veggie burger. Serve them with your favorite tip—hummus, tahini, the zucchini-based dressing on page 131, or ketchup, if you please. I particularly like the simple honey mustard dipping sauce below.

2 small or 1 large heads broccoli, preferably with plenty of stem

3 to 4 tablespoons olive oil

Salt

Freshly ground black pepper

HONEY MUSTARD SAUCE

2 tablespoons apple cider vinegar

2 tablespoons honey

2 tablespoons whole-grain mustard

1 garlic clove, finely minced

¼ teaspoon crushed red pepper flakes

½ teaspoon salt

3 tablespoons olive oil

1. Preheat the oven to 450°F (230°C). Place a rack in the top third of the oven.

2. Trim off any woody parts from the ends of the broccoli stem. Break the florets off as close to the stalk as possible, and trim down as needed to make them bite-size, but aiming to keep the pieces as long and skinny. (It's also fine to have short, chunky broccoli florets; they just won't resemble french fries.) Use a vegetable peeler to remove the fibrous outer layer of skin on the stalks, and then slice them about ¼-inch (6 mm) thick on a steep bias. Combine the broccoli with the oil, several pinches of salt, and a few grinds of pepper in a mixing bowl and toss to thoroughly coat, then spread in an even layer on a baking sheet.

3. Transfer to the oven and roast on the top rack until the florets are crispy and charred, and the stems are just tender and slightly blistered, 7 to 10 minutes.

4. Meanwhile, whisk together the vinegar, honey, mustard, garlic, red pepper flakes, and salt in a small bowl, then whisk in the oil until emulsified. Season with additional salt.

5. Serve the broccoli warm or at room temperature, with sauce on the side for dipping.

Rutabaga Fries Ⓥ ⒼⒻ

Makes 4 servings

Unless you live in the South or shop in a store that carries a wide variety of somewhat less-familiar produce, rutabagas may be hard to come by. They are yellow-fleshed, slightly sweet, turnip-like root vegetables that have a waxy exterior (which is sometimes pink- or purple-hued). If and when you have some, be sure to make these fries. They made me fall in love with the vegetable.

3 tablespoons olive oil, plus more for greasing

2 rutabagas

2 teaspoons potato starch or cornstarch

1 teaspoon salt

1. Preheat the oven to 450°F (230°C). Lightly oil a large baking sheet.

2. Slice off the top and bottom of the rutabagas so that they will rest flat on a cutting board. Then cut off the skin with a sharp paring knife or chef's knife by cutting against the curve of the flesh. (A vegetable peeler unfortunately doesn't cut thickly enough to scrape off all the skin.) Cut into ¼-inch (6 mm) matchsticks (see page 139).

3. Toss the potato starch with the rutabagas, then add the remaining oil and the salt.

4. Spread the rutabagas on the prepared baking sheet. Bake, flipping twice, for 25 to 30 minutes, until crispy on the outside and tender on the inside. Remove with a metal spatula and toss with additional salt to taste.

DO AHEAD: Cut rutabagas into matchsticks and keep covered with fresh water

Condiments and Toppings

Condiments and toppings are much more than an afterthought to a veggie burger, but as with side dishes, they need not be complicated or fussy. A bottle of sriracha and a jar of mustard within reach may be all that is needed for a movie night, whereas you'll be willing to trouble yourself if you're cooking for a more elaborate occasion.

I like to offer up a few of the following (along with toasted burger buns) whenever I am serving veggie burgers.

- **Thinly sliced tomato**

- **Thinly sliced red onion**

- **Crisp lettuce leaves, such as Bibb, romaine, red-leaf, or green-leaf**

- **Radish slices**

- **Cucumber slices**

- **Avocado slices**

- **Ketchup**

- **Mustard, whole-grain or Dijon**

- **Sriracha or other hot sauce**

- **Cheese (white cheddar, Swiss, Gruyère) and vegan soy cheese**

Here are some condiments that require a bit more advance planning.

- **Caramelized onions (see Tuscan White Bean Burgers, page 40)**

- **Roasted garlic (see Tuscan White Bean Burgers, page 40), mashed into a spread**

- **Hummus**

- **Olive tapenade (see headnote on page 134)**

- **Pesto: basil, mint, cilantro, or parsley, to name a few**

The condiments and toppings included in this chapter show up regularly at my table. My Quick Pickles (page 151) are the easiest, most delicious pickles I've ever tasted; they never last very long. The Quick-Pickled Red Onions (page 156) are a snap to make as well and are a surprising, welcome addition to almost any veggie burger. And one of the Four Simple Yogurt Sauces (pages 162–63) make delicious spreads for the burgers as well as dipping sauces for crudités and french fries.

Quick Pickles

Makes 1 quart (1 L)

These pickles have a clean flavor and are crisp—which is where so many other pickles fall short for me. Also, they are very easy. Make them when the farmers market or your local grocer is overflowing with Kirbys, or use any other cucumber you have on hand.

**4 small Kirby cucumbers, or
2 conventional cucumbers**

**2 tablespoons plus ½ teaspoon
kosher salt**

½ cup (120 ml) cider vinegar

2 tablespoons sugar

**3 garlic cloves, crushed and
peeled**

1 teaspoon black peppercorns

1 teaspoon mustard seeds

1. Cut the cucumbers into whatever shape you please. I prefer ¼-inch (6 mm) thick rounds cut on the bias. Toss with 2 tablespoons of the salt and place in a colander. Let stand for 30 minutes to 2 hours. Rinse thoroughly under running cold water, and gently blot dry.

2. Pack the cucumbers into a sterilized 1-quart (1 L) jar or divide between a few smaller jars.

3. Combine the vinegar, sugar, garlic, peppercorns, mustard seeds, and the remaining salt in a tall measuring glass and stir until the sugar and salt has dissolved. Then pour over the cucumbers. If they aren't submerged, add cold water to cover. These can be kept, refrigerated, for about 2 weeks; the flavors of the garlic and other aromatics will become stronger over time.

VARIATIONS: Other Aromatics

- Add 2 sprigs of fresh thyme with the garlic, peppercorns, and mustard seeds.

- Omit the mustard seeds and add 1 dried chile pepper and 1 star anise with the garlic and peppercorns.

- Omit the mustard seeds and garlic; add 1 bay leaf, 1 sprig of thyme, and 1 cinnamon stick with the peppercorns.

Frizzled Shallots Ⓥ ⑰

Makes 1½ cups (about 360 ml)

These crispy, savory fried shallots are an unexpected but welcome addition to veggie burgers. I especially like them on Curried Eggplant and Tomato Burgers (page 86). In the absence of shallots, use a small white or red onion, sliced as thinly as possible. The method here is one I came to learn later in my career: you'll begin with cold oil, which cooks the shallots gradually, and results in more even brownness.

8 shallots

Peanut, canola, or vegetable oil, for frying

Salt

1. Peel the shallots and carefully slice them into ⅛-inch-thick (3 mm) rings. (If you have a mandoline, this is a good opportunity to use it.)

2. Heat ½ inch (1.25 cm) oil in a heavy-bottomed sauté pan or saucepan over medium heat. Add the shallots. Stir gently until they begin to turn a golden-red color and turn crisp, usually about 8 to 10 minutes, though let your senses be your guide. Watch carefully toward the end, because once they begin to redden, they can easily brown and burn. Line a plate or baking sheet with paper towel or paper bags, and transfer the shallots from the oil with a slotted spoon. Sprinkle liberally with salt. These are best when freshly cooked, but stored in an airtight container, the shallots will keep for up to 3 days.

Beet Pickles ⓥ ⓖ

Makes about 1 quart (1 L)

I learned from my husband, Vincent, who's Australian, that in his home country a thick slice of pickled beet is extremely popular as a burger topping. I was skeptical, particularly with veggie burgers, worried they might be too sweet, but when sliced thin and pickled in something bracing rather than overly sweet, they add a lot of distinction to a burger or sandwich. When sandwiching on burger buns, arrange them underneath the burger. They're easier to cut through with your teeth that way.

2 medium beets, peeled

½ cup (120 ml) apple cider vinegar or rice vinegar

1 tablespoon sugar

1½ teaspoons kosher salt

1. Using a mandoline or working carefully with a sharp chef's knife, slice the beets into rounds about ⅛-inch (3 mm) thick. (Your hands will be temporarily stained, but I find that it always washes off faster than I expect.)

2. Bring a saucepan of water to boil, season with salt, then add the beets. Parcook them until just tender and certainly not mushy, usually just 5 to 8 minutes. Drain and transfer to a sterilized wide-mouthed jar or other container that comes with a lid.

3. In the saucepan, combine ½ cup (120 ml) water water with the vinegar, sugar, and salt and heat until the solids dissolve. Pour the mixture over the beets, ensuring that they're submerged and adding equal parts vinegar and water as needed. Allow to cool, then seal and store in the fridge overnight before serving.

Quick-Pickled Red Onions Ⓥ 🄶

Makes 1½ cups (about 360 ml)

Pickled onions are a great addition to almost any burger, sandwich, or salad, adding a bracing contrast to rich foods and strong flavors. Use any light-colored vinegar you prefer: red or white wine vinegar, plain white vinegar, rice vinegar, and cider vinegar all work very well.

1 cup (240 ml) cold water

⅔ cup (160 ml) vinegar (see headnote)

1 teaspoon kosher salt

1 teaspoon sugar

1 large or 2 small red onions, sliced into ⅛-inch-thick (3 mm) rings

In a small saucepan, combine the cold water, vinegar, salt, and sugar. Place over medium heat and bring to a simmer. Add the onions. As the mixture comes back to heat, the onions will collapse and become submerged in the liquid, which will only take a few minutes. Remove from the heat and allow to cool, then transfer to a sterilized lidded container and store in the refrigerator for up to 2 weeks.

Spiced Tomato Relish Ⓥ ⒼⒻ

Makes ½ cup (about 120 ml)

Pair this relish with any curry spiced burger. It has ketchup vibes, as well as salsa vibes, but tastes like neither of the two. It's great with many of the bean-based burgers in this book—particularly the Easy Bean Burgers (page 31), or the Spinach-Chickpea Burgers (page 81), as well as the Curried Eggplant and Tomato Burgers (page 86).

1 cup (150 g) cherry tomatoes

3 tablespoons minced cilantro

2 tablespoons finely minced red onion

Squeeze of fresh lime juice

1 teaspoon garam masala

½ teaspoon coriander

Salt

1. Preheat the oven to 450°F (230°C). Line a small baking sheet with aluminum foil.

2. Place the tomatoes on the prepared baking sheet. Roast for 20 minutes, stirring every 5 minutes, until they begin to shrivel or burst. Allow to cool.

3. Coarsely chop the tomatoes and transfer to a mixing bowl. Add the cilantro, onion, lemon juice, garam masala, coriander, and salt to taste. Adjust seasonings. This relish will keep in an airtight container in the refrigerator for 4 to 5 days.

Pomegranate-Sesame Sauce Ⓥ ⒼⒻ

Makes ¼ cup (about 60 ml)

Pomegranate molasses is nothing more than reduced pomegranate juice, and it's delicious in sauces and marinades and by itself as a drizzle over ice cream and oatmeal. It also shows up in the Quinoa, Red Bean, and Walnut Burgers (page 50). It packs a puckering punch in this recipe; a little bit of the sauce goes a long way. Many grocery stores now carry pomegranate molasses, but you may need to head to a specialty store.

¼ cup (84 g) pomegranate molasses

¼ cup (60 ml) soy sauce or tamari (GF)

1 tablespoon molasses

1 teaspoon sesame oil

Combine the pomegranate molasses, soy sauce, molasses, and sesame oil in a small saucepan. Cook over low heat, stirring occasionally, until reduced by half, 6 to 8 minutes. It will thicken as it cools. This sauce will keep in the refrigerator for up to 2 weeks.

Sweet Sesame Glaze Ⓥ ⒼⒻ

Makes ½ cup (about 120 ml)

This glaze is another great use for pomogranate molasses. Use it as a base for panfried tofu or a stir-fry sauce, or with the Tofu and Chard Burgers (page 96) or the Tofu-Mushroom Burgers (page 104). The honey lends a surprising savory depth.

½ cup (120 ml) soy sauce or tamari (GF)

1 tablespoon toasted sesame oil

2 teaspoons agave nectar or 1 tablespoon honey

½ teaspoon pomegranate molasses

2 tablespoons sesame seeds

2 tablespoons thinly sliced scallions (including 1 inch/2.5 cm of the dark green parts)

Combine the soy sauce, sesame oil, agave, and pomegranate molasses in a small saucepan and cook over medium heat, swirling the pan often, until slightly reduced, about 5 minutes. Remove from the heat, stir in the sesame seeds, and allow to cool to room temperature; it will thicken slightly as it cools. The sauce will keep in an airtight container in the refrigerator for up to a week. Stir in the scallions just before serving.

Mango BBQ Sauce Ⓥ ⒼⒻ

Makes 2 cups (about 480 ml)

This is a great everyday barbecue sauce for all kinds of burgers. It also works well as a dipping sauce for French fries. If you'd like, amp up the heat by adding a bit more cayenne and chili powder. The flavors improve after a day or two, so it's best to make it in advance.

1 cup (235 g) ketchup (GF)

¾ cup (240 g) mango chutney

½ cup (120 ml) plus 1 tablespoon cider vinegar

2 teaspoons Dijon mustard (GF)

1 teaspoon chili powder

1 teaspoon liquid smoke

1 teaspoon molasses

2 garlic cloves, minced

¼ teaspoon cayenne pepper

1. Combine the ketchup, chutney, vinegar, mustard, chili powder, liquid smoke, molasses, garlic, and cayenne in a medium saucepan. Bring to a boil, reduce to medium, and cook until slightly reduced and thickened, 30 to 40 minutes.

2. Transfer to the bowl of a food processor or blender and purée. Alternatively, purée with an immersion blender. Allow to cool, then refrigerate until ready to use. The sauce will keep in an airtight container in the refrigerator for up to 2 weeks.

Charred Scallion Relish Ⓥ ⒼⒻ

Makes about 1½ cups (350 ml)

In vegetarian cooking, charred scallions add a significant depth of flavor and complexity, especially for such a straightforward vegetable and easy technique. This is a relish that's excellent on veggie burgers or to use as a dip for fries or chips. It's quite not as punchy as you might expect but is instead a bit rich and surprisingly creamy, with a smoky back note. Once you have some on hand, you'll find all kinds of ways to use it—on grain bowls, sandwiches and wraps, and as a dip for crackers or crudités.

1 bunch scallions, roots and tips trimmed

5 tablespoons olive oil

Salt

1 garlic clove

1 tablespoon fresh lemon juice

1 tablespoon white wine vinegar

1 teaspoon honey, or 1½ teaspoons maple syrup

¼ teaspoon crushed red pepper flakes

1 cup (20 g) basil or mint leaves, minced

1. Cut the scallions in half widthwise, so they all fit in a skillet. Heat a skillet over medium-high heat. Add 2 tablespoons of the oil, then the scallions and a pinch of salt, spreading the scallions in a single layer as best as you can. Sear them on both sides until charred and the white parts are tender, 6 to 8 minutes; you'll want to press down on them periodically using a spatula, to encourage them to char. Transfer to a cutting board and allow to cool until safe to handle, then chop to a coarse mash.

2. On a cutting board, smash the garlic with the side of a chef's knife and sprinkle with a big pinch of salt. Mince and mash the garlic, pressing it down and fanning it out over your cutting board, over and over until it becomes garlic paste. Transfer to a medium bowl. Add the lemon juice, vinegar, honey, red pepper flakes, and the remaining oil and whisk until combined. Stir in the scallions and the basil. (Alternatively, combine this mixture in a mini food processor or use a bullet-style blender to process, for a creamier consistency.) Adjust salt to taste. This relish will keep in an airtight container for about 3 days.

Four Simple Yogurt Sauces GF

Plain yogurt is a refreshing base for any number of savory and sweet sauces, particularly as an alternate to mayo-based sauces. I prefer Greek-style drained yogurt because it doesn't split from the whey when left to sit, and also because of its rich, luxuriant texture. But these recipes are equally delicious with undrained yogurt, which you can drain yourself if you please (see page 165). All these recipes work both as spreads for burgers and sandwiches and as dipping sauces for chips and fries. The sauces can be made a few hours in advance. The whey may separate, in which case just stir until combined and smooth.

Curried Yogurt Sauce GF

Makes 1 cup (about 285 g)

1 cup (285 g) Greek-style
    plain yogurt
2 tablespoons finely minced
    cilantro
2 teaspoons lime juice
2 teaspoons curry powder
1 teaspoon coriander
½ teaspoon salt
Pinch of cayenne pepper
Pinch of sugar or drizzle of honey

Combine the yogurt, cilantro, lime juice, curry powder, coriander, salt, cayenne, and sugar. Adjust seasonings.

Almond Yogurt Sauce GF

Makes 1¼ cups (about 356 g)

¾ cup (214 g) Greek-style
    plain yogurt
½ cup (125 g) almond butter
2 tablespoons finely minced
    fresh parsley
1 teaspoon ground cardamom
½ teaspoon honey
¼ teaspoon salt

Combine the yogurt, almond butter, parsley, cardamon, honey, and salt. Adjust seasonings.

Tahini Yogurt Sauce GF

Makes 1¼ cups (about 356 g)

¾ cup (214 g) Greek-style
   plain yogurt

½ cup (120 ml) tahini

2 tablespoons finely minced
   fresh parsley

1 garlic clove, minced

1 teaspoon lemon juice

½ teaspoon ground cumin

¼ teaspoon salt

Dash of hot sauce

Combine the yogurt, tahini,
parsley, garlic, lemon juice,
cumin, salt, and hot sauce.
Adjust seasonings.

Cucumber Yogurt Sauce GF

Makes 1¼ cups (about 356 g)

½ red onion, minced

2 teaspoons lemon juice

½ teaspoon salt

1 small cucumber, grated or finely chopped

1 cup (285 g) Greek-style plain yogurt

¼ cup (15 g) chopped fresh mint, loosely packed

1 garlic clove, minced

Pinch of cayenne pepper

Combine the onion, lemon juice, and salt in a medium
bowl and let stand for a few minutes. Add the
cucumber, yogurt, mint, garlic, and cayenne. Adjust
seasonings.

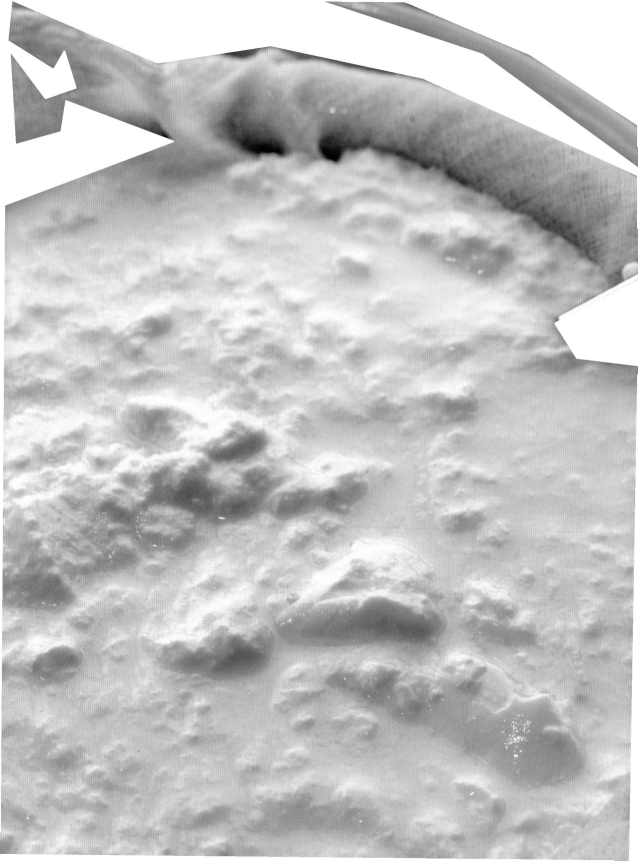

DRAIN YOUR OWN YOGURT

If you can't find Greek-style yogurt, it's very easy to drain plain yogurt yourself in order to achieve the thickness that is the hallmark of the Greek style. Some yogurts have added gelatins and emulsifiers that prevent the whey from separating; you'll need to make sure to use a yogurt that does not include these. Stir the yogurt until smooth. Line a sieve or colander with a triple layer of cheesecloth, then transfer the yogurt in it. Allow to drain for 2 to 4 hours, until desired thickness is reached. You can even make yogurt cheese by tying the cheesecloth into a little satchel hung over a wooden spoon, allowing the yogurt to drain into a bowl overnight in the refrigerator.

Acknowledgments

First and foremost, thank you to publisher and original editor, Matthew Lore, who had the idea for this cookbook and its reissue, and who trusted that I was capable of executing it when I had very little demonstrated experience.

Thank you to the incredibly talented team at The Experiment who published the original edition in 2010, proceeded to enthusiastically support it for over a decade, and then fully revitalized it with this gorgeous new edition—especially Peter Burri, Danica Donovan, Olivia Peluso, Jack Palmer, Karen Giangreco, and Nicholas Cizek. Thank you, Beth Bugler, for the stunning new design and cover and for overseeing the fresh look.

Thank you photographer Evi Abeler and food stylist Albane Sharrard for the terrific new photographs and for welcoming me into the shoot for a day. Thank you, Christina Heaston, for your original photographs and a very memorable baptism-by-fire photo shoot.

Thank you to the many supporters of my veggie burger endeavors over the years. In particular, thank you, Dave Liatti, Lalit Chopra, Jina Kim, and An Nuyen, who were instrumental in helping create Made by Lukas. Thank you, Martha Rose Shulman, Melissa Clark, Jeff Gordinier, Tejal Rao, Ben Mims, Chitra Agrawal, Cathy Erway, and Alicia Kennedy, for supporting my work and advancing the discourse.

Thank you always to my family: my husband, Vincent; my brother and his wife, Max and Casady Volger; my late grandfather, Glen Scott; my stepmom, Pam Robinson; and especially my dad, Ron Volger, my first editor, whose kitchen got a serious workout during this book's original photo shoot. You all continue to make me feel very lucky.

Resources

The following cookbooks have been very helpful sources of inspiration and information.

Bronski, Kelli, and Peter Bronski. *Artisanal Gluten-Free Cooking.* New York: The Experiment, 2009.

Dornenburg, Andrew, and Karen Page. *The Flavor Bible.* New York: Little, Brown, 2008.

Jaffrey, Madhur. *Madhur Jaffrey's World Vegetarian.* New York: Clarkson Potter, 2002.

Madison, Deborah. *Vegetarian Cooking for Everyone.* New York: Broadway Books, 1997.

Moskowitz, Isa Chandra. *Vegan with a Vengeance.* New York: Marlowe & Company, 2005.

Moskowitz, Isa Chandra, and Terry Hope Romero. *Veganomicon.* New York: Da Capo, 2007.

Swanson, Heidi. *Super Natural Cooking.* Berkeley, CA: Celestial Arts, 2007.

Index

Page numbers in *italics* refer to photos.

H

hazelnuts
    Barley Salad with Beets and Goat Cheese, *136*, 137
    Beet and Hazelnut Burgers, 78–79, *78–79*
herbs, leftover, 38–39, *38–39*
honey, 142, *143*

K

kale
    Kale and Quinoa Burgers, *42*, 42–43
    Raw Kale Salad with Apples and Candied Walnuts, 132
    Sweet Potato Burgers with Lentils and Kale, 82–83, *82–83*

L

leeks
    Cashew-Leek Burgers with Bulgur and Lentils, *46*, 46–47
    cleaning, 48, *48*
leftovers, 25, 38–39, *38–39*
lentils
    about, 28, *29*
    Cashew-Leek Burgers with Bulgur and Lentils, *46*, 46–47
    Red Lentil and Celeriac Burgers, 52–53, *53*
    Spiced Lentil Burgers, 32–33, *33*
    Sweet Potato Burgers with Lentils and Kale, 82–83, *82–83*
lettuce, *130*, 131

M

Mango BBQ Sauce
    recipe, 159
    Seitan Burgers with Mango BBQ Sauce, 98–99, *99*
meat grinders, 22
mixers, stand, 108
mushrooms
    Best Portobello Burgers, 62–63, *63*

"Garden" Burgers, 101
    Mushroom Burgers with Barley, 68, *69*
    Seitan Burgers with Mango BBQ Sauce, 98–99, *99*
    Tofu-Mushroom Burgers, 104, *105*
    Tortilla-Crusted Stuffed Portobello Burgers, 71
mustard, 142, *143*

O

olives, kalamata
    Black Olive and Roasted Potato Salad with Arugula, 134, *135*
    Tuscan White Bean Burgers, 40–41, *40–41*
onions, 156, *157*
oranges, *122*, 123

P

panfrying, 23
pans, nonstick oven-safe sauté, 22
parsnips, *72*, 73
peanut butter, *66*, 67
peppers
    Chipotle Black Bean Burgers, 92, *93*
    Roasted Corn Salad, 128, *129*
pineapple, *102*, 103
Pomegranate-Sesame Sauce, 158
potatoes
    Black Olive and Roasted Potato Salad with Arugula, 134, *135*
    Classic Baked Fries, 138, *138*
    Curried Eggplant and Tomato Burgers, 86, *87*
    cutting into fries, 139, *139*
    Mushroom Burgers with Barley, 68, *69*
    See also sweet potatoes
potato mashers, 20
Pretzel Rolls, 114–15, *115*
Pub Grub Veggie Burgers, 55, *55*